UNLEASH THE TIGER!

FOR ORGANIZATIONAL HIGH PERFORMANCE

The Fundamentals

By Dr. Simmie A. Adams

COPYRIGHT AND DISCLAIMER

This material is copyrighted. No part, in whole or in part, may be reproduced by any process, or any other exclusive right exercised, without the written permission of Dr. Simmie A. Adams © 2018

Copyright © 2012018 Simmie A. Adams
All rights reserved.
ISBN-10: 173205410X
ISBN-13: 978-1-7320541-0-3

Simmie A. Adams

Published by:

The Consortium of Scientific Practitioners

11656 Soldier's Trail

Bealeton, VA 22712

Tel: 1 910 574 7874

Website: www.csp-llc.org

DISCLAIMER AND/OR LEGAL NOTICES:

While every attempt has been made to verify information provided in this book, the author assumes no responsibility for any errors, omissions, or inaccuracies.

Any slights of people or organizations are unintentional. If advice concerning legal or related matters is needed, the services of a qualified professional should be sought. This book is not intended as a source of legal or accounting advice. You should be aware of any laws which govern business transactions or other business practices in your state or province.

Any reference or any perceived resemblance or implication to any persons or business, whether living or deceased, existing or defunct, is purely coincidental.

PRINTED IN THE USA

Foreword

I had the distinct pleasure and honor of serving with Dr. Adams as a consultant to the National Geospatial Intelligence Agency. From our daily interactions, I grew to appreciate and value Dr. Adams' distinguished service to our great nation. He is a superb military leader and renowned academic in organizational performance. He has a wealth of military leadership experience having served in the US Army both in times of peace and during contingency operations across the globe. In addition to his impeccable military service, Dr. Adams has researched and written a myriad of articles on High Performing Organizations.

During our time together as consultants, we often shared our notes and observations on high performing organizations. Having spent many hours in spirited debates with Dr. Adams on the essence of HPOs, I was delighted to learn of his compilation of his research found in the pages to follow. Dr. Adams was a Master Parachutist while serving in the Army—he is an expert having safely descended the skies on countless jumps out of 'perfectly good airplanes'. At the same time, he studied and learned how to ascend the military ranks and elevate unit performance within the Special Operations community—the elite of our Armed Forces.

I share and endorse the premise of Dr. Adams' extensive research that **any** and **all** organizations have the potential to climb to the stratosphere of performance provided the environment is founded on trust and respect coupled with a strong dose of servant leadership resident at all levels. Much like Dr. Adams, I too have served in a number of organizations at all levels within the Department of Defense and on two separate occasions over a three-decade career in uniform experienced the magic elixir needed to develop an average performing unit into a qualified HPO. To be sure, Dr. Adams' research hits the target!

For all who are seeking to improve your leadership skills or looking to take your organization to unimaginable heights of excellence, you will surely benefit from Dr. Adams' sage advice. This book provides a wonderful opportunity to 'take the tiger by the tail' and drive extraordinary results regardless of whether you are in the military, public sector or in private industry.

There is much to be gained through this insightful journey into the world of high performing organizations—Aim High!

Joseph S. Ward, Jr.
Major General, USAF (Ret.)
One Nation Under God

This page left blank intentionally.

Prelude

In today's dynamic business world, organizations must adapt, overcome, and improvise to meet quickly and efficiently the pressures and demands of a modern environment. As James Duderstadt summarized, "We face a future in which permanence and stability become less important than flexibility and creativity, in which one of the few certainties will be the presence of continual change."[1] Organizations must rely on the knowledge, skills, and experience of a wide range of people to solve multifaceted problems, make good decisions, and deliver effective solutions to achieve successfully their strategic vision.

The current environment is one of shrinking revenues and increased costs and expenditures, a heightened need exists for value added efforts focused on increasing organizational performance and subsequently increasing business profits. The road to increased organization profits is built on an organizational foundation supporting, reinforcing, and even demanding improved performance.

The question to answer is "What does an organization have to do to have its name analogous with high performance?" Prior to answering the question, one must be prepared to explain the concept of what does it mean to be a high performance organization. A critical analysis is essential to one's understanding of the end state for which the organization is striving. One must be perceptive of *what is a high performance organization?* To grasp this concept, a reverse engineering process is an effective means to get to the end.

Prior to beginning the dismantling process, one should understand the house. In this case, the house is the high performance organization. A thorough exploration of the house is in order to determine why the organization is considered high performance.

Now, the house needs to be brought down brick by brick. Each brick closely examined as to its texture, smell, weight, density, and composition. Each brick needs to be studied. In addition, what is holding each brick to other bricks? The mortar or concrete needs to be scrutinized completely. The bricks and concrete are analogous to concepts and theories respectively. Without an understanding of common terms and concepts as well as the theories behind them, no one will be speaking the same language.

This situation would be like putting two people in a room where one speaks Chinese and the other Arabic. This point is made, not at the detriment of any culture, but rather by understanding, these are two extremely difficult and distinct languages. They sound nothing alike and there is no way on this green earth these two individuals are going to easily understand each other. At best,

---

[1] Duderstadt, J. (2000; p35). *A university for the 21st century*. Ann Arbor, MI: University of Michigan Press.

maybe, they may be able to communicate with a few rudimentary hand and facial gestures. The learning objective is to ensure everyone is speaking the same language and has an understanding of what comprises a house or in this case a high performance organization. In other words, what are the concepts and theories behind high performance organizations? The concepts and theories bring to life their applicability. Without applicability, concepts and theories mean nothing.

As all the mortar and concrete is chipped away and every brick is removed and nicely placed on the side, the foundation remains. Here lies the critical corner stone, the building blocks upon which the whole house rests. These are the blocks ensuring all else is firm and steady. If an organization, like a house, does not have these blocks, its foundation is weak and there is a propensity for the organization to fall. An organization, like a house, built on sand will surely shift and collapse. However, if the organization is built on a bed of rock, it will stand fast against the raging storm and will last against the sands of time. The blocks, spoken of, are the critical elements required and displayed by all high performance organizations. These blocks are the senior leaders' goals and objectives to strive for during the journey to developing a high performance organization. These blocks must exist before the brick and mortar gets placed.

Now, before a single step of the journey can be initiated, before a single foundational block is laid, prior to the mixing of any mortar or concrete, and the laying of even one brick, an architectural-blueprint must exist. At this point in the reverse engineering process, the question, *what does an organization have to do to have its name analogous with high performance?* is answered. The response presents what it takes for an organization to become high performing.

Finally, the concept for the house needs to be developed. The question, *where am I now?* is answered. Before any journey begins, a start point must be determined. Without knowing where one is, creating a path to the desired result, or location, is challenging. The organization must assess where they are in reference to where they want to be. This activity is a fact-finding mission. They need to peel the proverbial organizational onion.

Does the organization have any of the attributes of high performance? If so, in what quantities do they exist? If not, what attributes do they have and are they complimentary to the desired attributes?

To answer these questions by using a medical model, one would be hesitant to use a surgeon who wants to operate without having x-rays, MRIs, laboratory work, and such done so to determine exactly what surgical procedure to perform. Assessments should be conducted to determine exactly how the organization is performing. Once the assessments are conducted, the statistical analysis performed, and the conclusions drawn, the plan can be devised and initiated. The path the organization is going to travel in its journey to high performance is determined.

One can easily observe how organizational high performance is crucial just by watching the real life drama of organization and team performance in combat operations within Afghanistan or Iraq. Organizational performance, in those specific work environments, has a life or death consequence. Organizations, which fail to maximize their competitive advantage, may well find themselves in a non-competitive situation. Organizational performance is just as critical in any environment. An organization may die if they are performing poorly. Unfortunately, this fact seems to be unknown to some senior leaders.

Therefore, the battle cry is:

High performance is the way to go!

Let the journey begin!

Unleash the Tiger™!

This page left blank intentionally.

Table of Contents

Foreword .... *i*

Prelude .... *iii*

Chapter 1: Prologue *1*
INTRODUCTION 1
What is an organization? 1

What is a high performance organization? 1

FUNDAMENTALS OF ORGANIZATIONAL HIGH PERFORMANCE 2
The Management System 2

The Business Model 2

The Leadership Standard 3

The Organizational Science 3

The Organizational Action Research Schemata 5

CONCLUSION 6

Chapter 2: The Management System *7*
INTRODUCTION 7
PROGRAMS 8
Strategic Management 8

Operations Management 10

Resource Management 11

Performance Management 11

Communications Management 15

CONCLUSION 19

Chapter 3: The Business Model *21*
INTRODUCTION 21
THE BUSINESS MODEL 21
Core Values and Goals 22

Strategy 22

Structure 23

Culture 23

Leadership 24

People (Human Capital) 24

Skills 25

Work Processes 25

  Systems 26

  Environment 27

 Conclusion 27

Chapter 4: The Leadership Standard *31*
 Introduction 31
 Leadership 32
  Defined 32
  Types and Levels 33
 Styles 35
  Servant Leadership (Foundational) 35
  Environmental Leadership (Strategic Leadership Level) 40
  Participative Leadership (Organizational Leadership Level) 44
  Situational Leadership (Direct Leadership Level) 47
 Conclusion 51

Chapter 5: The Organizational Science *54*
 Introduction 54
  The Organization 56
  The Psychology 57
  The Biology 59
  The Physics 61
  The Science 61
 The Science of Psychology 62
  Theory of Cognitive Psychology 62
  Theory of Behavioral Psychology 64
  Theory of Affective Psychology 66
  Theory of Social Psychology 67
  Theory of Humanistic Psychology 68
 The Science of Biology 69
  Theory of Cells 69
  Theory of Evolution 70
  Theory of Genetics 71
  Theory of Homeostasis 72
  Theory of Energy 72
  Theory of Systems 73
  Theory of Complex Adaptive Social Systems 74

    Theory of Neuroscience 76
  THE SCIENCE OF PHYSICS 88
    Theory of Dynamical Systems 88
    Theory of Chaos 89
    Theory of Classical Mechanics 90
    Zeroth Law of Thermodynamics (Thermal Equilibrium) 93
    First Law of Thermodynamics 94
    Second Law of Thermodynamics 97
    Third Law of Thermodynamics 100
    Law of the Conservation of Momentum 101
    Law of Gravity 105
  CONCLUSION 107

Chapter 6: The Organizational Action Research Schemata *109*
  INTRODUCTION 109
  THE SCHEMATA 114
    Schema 1: Engagement 114
    Schema 2: Diagnosis 114
    Schema 3: Planning 115
    Schema 4: Implementation 115
    Schema 5: Reflection 116
    Schema 6: Disengagement 116
    Schema 7: Epilogue 116
  CONCLUSION 117

Chapter 7: Epilogue *119*
  INTRODUCTION 119
  FUNDAMENTALS OF ORGANIZATIONAL HIGH PERFORMANCE 119
    The Management System 119
    The Business Model 120
    The Leadership Standard 120
    The Organizational Science 121
    The Organizational Action Research Schemata 121
  CONCLUSION 122

Success Overture *125*
  OVERVIEW 125
  DEVELOPING HIGH PERFORMANCE ORGANIZATIONS 125
  DEVELOPING HIGH PERFORMANCE TEAMS 129
  DEVELOPING HIGH PERFORMANCE INDIVIDUALS 131

DEVELOPING HIGH PERFORMANCE LEADERS	132
Glossary	*134*
About the Author	*136*

Chapter 1:
Prologue

Introduction

What is an organization?

Organizations consist of many different types of people, who may have different styles and who work with others they may not normally interact with on a routine basis. Organizations involve individuals, brought together, from different backgrounds and orientations. Its dynamics can prove perplexing and challenging because the members may have different values, attitudes, and expectations. Many organizations may take on their own personality and culture.

What is a high performance organization?

The Society of Human Resource Management defines a high performance organization (HPO) as a responsive organization where people, processes, and technology are aligned fully to produce exceptional results, experience rapid growth, and sustain its competitive advantage as compared to its competitors.[2]

Another HPO definition states it is an entity that achieves financial results that are better than those of its peer group over a longer period of time, by:[3]

- being able to react quickly and adapt well to changes
- managing for the longer term
- setting up an integrated and aligned management structure
- continuously improving its core capabilities
- truly treating the employees as its main asset

By drawing a conclusion from the above definitions and synthesizing from some other definitions, a high performance organization is comprised of one or more teams, each consisting of two or more individuals, with all having complementary skills, interests, and beliefs brought together for coordinated activities to achieve a higher goal. The teams interact cooperatively and adaptively in pursuit of shared and valued objectives. Additionally, the teams are committed to a common organizational purpose, work toward shared and meaningful performance goals, and take approaches for which they are mutually accountable. The organization's

---

[2] Society for Human Resource Management (2007). *Business literacy glossary of terms*. Retrieved on April 3, 2012, from http://www.shrm.org

[3] De Waal, A. (2007; p3). *The characteristics of a high performance organization.* Retrieved on August 24, 2016, from http://www.andredewall.eu/pdf2007/HPO-BSS2007.pdf

members have clearly defined and differentiated roles and responsibilities, hold task-relevant knowledge, and are interdependent.[4][5][6]

Fundamentals of Organizational High Performance

The Management System

A Management System is foundational to organizational high performance as it enables over the horizon planning by incorporating best practices to effectively lead and manage high-performing organizations. Additionally, the system enables an organization's enduring core functions to maintain their competitive advantage and unique value contributions to their stakeholders. The System's strength lies in its utilization of five distinct, but interrelated management programs:

- Strategic Management
- Operations Management
- Resource Management
- Performance Management
- Communications Management

Applying this Management System to an organization ensures it has a clear procedural picture to develop or refine who they are, where they are going, and how they will get there from a transformational, collaborative, and integrative perspective. The system is structured around the best practices utilized to effectively lead and manage high-performance organizations.

The Business Model

The business model presents information concerning the holistic, high performing organizational workplace environment.

The climate of a high performing organizational workplace environment should be one that creates a feeling of belonging while valuing the human diversity of the organization through trust and respect.[7] The Institute for Organizational Performance purports a positive-emotional workplace climate creates *more*

---

[4] Cannon-Bowers, J., Salas, E., & Converse, S. (1993). Shared mental models in expert team decision making. In J. Castellan Jr. (Ed.), *Current issues in individual and group decision-making* (pp. 221-246). Hillsdale, NJ: Erlbaum.

[5] Katzenbach, J., & Smith, D. (1993). *The wisdom of teams: Creating the high-performance organization.* Boston, MA: Harvard Business School.

[6] Morgan, B. B., Glickman, A. S., Woodward, E. A., Blaiwes, A. S., & Salas, E. (1986). *Measurement of team behaviors in a Navy environment* (Tech. Report No. NTSC TR-86-014). Orlando, FL: Naval Training Systems Center.

[7] Jennings, K. (n.d.). *Fostering a workplace climate for diversity.* Retrieved on November, 27, 2005 from http://www.arl.org/newsltr/185/foster.html.

engaged employees.[8] Employees that are more engaged will accomplish goals and objectives, be customer service focused, and increase the financial bottom line when the work environment is considered positive and in good health. The Army has for many years been concerned with the unit's climate. Before, during, and at the end of a unit commander's tenure, an equal opportunity advisor will survey the organization to bring to light the work climate of that organization. An environment that does not foster equal opportunity for everyone or embellishes on harassment of any type will not be tolerated in the military for it inhibits the critical good order and discipline that is required for a successful military unit. The IOP indicates the hub to a positive workplace climate is trust.[9]

Understanding and leveraging the business model information will enable an organization to drive toward and ultimately achieve high performance.

The Leadership Standard

The quality of the leadership has a direct correlation to the productivity of the organization. Leadership is "influencing people -- by providing purpose, direction, and motivation -- while operating to accomplish the mission and improving the organization."[10] These qualities of providing purpose, direction, and motivation dramatically influence employees to achieve organizational objectives directly correlate to the importance of leadership and its impact on performance. Maddux and Wingfield point out that leadership is team building.[11] If the organization is a team then the business will work as one to accomplish its goals. The end state accomplished will be greater that the individual sum of the parts.[12]

The Organizational Science

Albert Einstein stated, "Something deeply hidden had to be behind things."[13] The implication within the context of organizational high performance is there are influencing forces at work internal and external to an organization. Some of these

---

[8] IOP (n.d. a). *Increasing value for all stakeholders by improving the workplace climate*. Retrieved on November 27, 2005, from http://www.eqperformance.com/pdf/IOP_capabilities.pdf.

[9] IOP (n.d. b). *An organizational climate survey to improve performance*. Retrieved on November 27, 2005, from http://www.eqperformance.com/pdf/IOP_OVS.pdf.

[10] Department of the Army (1999; p4). *FM 22-100: Army Leadership -- Be, Know, Do*. Washington, DC: Department of the Army.

[11] Maddux, B., & Wingfield, B. (2003). *Team building: An exercise in leadership* (4th ed.). Menlo Park, NJ: Crisp Publications.

[12] Doren, D., McCutcheon, A., Evans, M., MacMillan, K., Hall, L., Pringle, D., Smith, S., & Valente, A. (September, 2004). Impact of the manager's span of control on leadership and performance. *Canadian Health Services Research Foundation Publication*. Retrieved on November 27, 2005 from http://www.chsrf.ca/final_research /ogc/pdf/doran2_final.pdf

[13] Einstein, A. (n.d.). *Autobiographical notes*. Retrieved on February 9, 2017, from http://www.quotes.net/ quote/9269

forces are promoting or advancing the organizational culture or change efforts whereas others are inhibiting or degenerating its culture or change efforts. If the forces are in equilibrium, then the organization will remain in homeostasis, the tendency toward a relatively stable balance between interdependent elements, especially as maintained by physiological processes. However, if the forces are imbalanced, then dependent upon what forces are dominate, the organization's culture will advance or degrade or will achieve or not achieve its desired future state.

Psychology, as championed through the American Psychology Association, is the science of understanding people from a perspective of their cognitions, behavior, and affections, equating to thoughts, actions, and emotions respectively. People are complex, adaptive systems. Because people comprise organizations, organizations are also complex, adaptive systems. There are numerous psychological paradigms; the more holistic ones, aligning to organizational high performance, fall under the realm of Social and Humanistic Psychology. Industrial and Organizational Psychology, as presented by the Society for Industrial and Organizational Psychology, via a scientific method, stitches the science of understanding people and the numerous psychological paradigms together. It does the stitching through the scientific study of the organizational work environment and applying the science to the organizational workplace and the issues facing individuals, teams, and organizations.

Biology is a natural science focused on studying life. Specifically, it is the study of the structure, function, growth, origin, evolution, and distribution of living organisms. The Theory of Systems, the Theory of Evolution, and the Theory of Complex Adaptive Social Systems emerged from the biological realm. There are numerous branches of biology; however, they tend to agree on a framework of five basic ideas in regards to living organisms. These five ideas are:[14]

- **Cell Theory**: There are three parts to cell theory — the cell is the basic unit of life, all living things are composed of cells, and all cells arise from pre-existing cells.
- **Energy**: All living things require energy, and energy flows between organisms and between organisms and the environment.
- **Heredity**: All living things have DNA and genetic information codes the structure and function of all cells.
- **Equilibrium**: All living things must maintain homeostasis, a state of balanced equilibrium between the organism and its environment.
- **Evolution**: This is the overall unifying concept of biology. Evolution is the change over time that is the engine of biological diversity.

---

[14] LiveScience. (n.d.). *What is biology? Framework of understanding.* Retrieved on March 1, 2017, from http://www.livescience.com/44549-what-is-biology.html

Physics is the science dealing with matter and energy and their interactions.[15] It is the universal laws utilized to understand and explain the physical processes and phenomena of a particular system. All systems have common cognitive, behavioral, and affective properties. The system of interest is the complex adaptive system, called the organization. The premise is basic laws of organizational nature exist through which to determine the performance of any organization.

Therefore, *The Organizational Science*, leading toward organizational high performance, presents the universal theories and laws of psychology, biology, and physics through which to explain how an organization foundationally operates. Through this understanding, these theories and laws can be utilized to create a valid plan designed to increase or enhance the organization's performance. These theories help us understand what promoting and inhibiting forces are at work, either overtly or covertly, within an organization and how these forces can be leveraged or minimized provides insight on how the organization can evolve and improve itself.

The Organizational Action Research Schemata

People want to be part of a high performing organization. Individually, people bring their collective blueprint to the organization. This blueprint is comprised of a blending of all their past and present attributes, which have shaped and defined the individual. The integration of all the attributes comprising of the individual blueprints as well as how well they function from an interrelationship standpoint creates the organizational blueprint.

Organizations, groups, sections, and teams comprise of individuals. From a systemic viewpoint, the organization is a function of its individualistic parts. Therefore, understanding the organization is accomplished through the study of the individuals comprising the organization. The phenomenon, when working at an optimum performance level, creates a greater product or service in a more efficient way. This organizational phenomenon could be described as an organizational person. By understanding the complexity of the individual parts and their blueprints, the organizational phenomenon, the organizational blueprint, begins to be understood. With understanding, the issue or situation inhibiting the organization's performance can be overcome.

The Organizational Action Research Schemata, as a foundational component of organizational high performance, incorporates studying organizational blueprints through also studying the individual blueprints comprising the organization. The study of the organization's blueprint provides insight into their maladaptive issues

---

[15] Merriam-Webster (n.d.). *Physics – Definition.* Retrieved on May 23, 2016, from
http://www.merriam-webster.com/dictionary/physics

or situations. This insight is illuminated with data related to such constructs as organizational characteristics, patterns, knowledge, skills, and values. The Organizational Action Research Schemata is the methodology assisting an organization toward high performance.

Conclusion

People comprise teams, teams comprise branches, branches comprise divisions, divisions comprise offices, offices comprise groups, and groups comprise organizations. Though the entities are different, they must work well together, like a well-built and oiled machine, as well as to be constantly learning and evolving to achieve high performance. Optimally, the organization strives to be high performing resulting in the highest level of revenue possible because of the exceptional customer satisfaction and experience.

As Stephen R. Covey says, one must keep the end in mind. With this statement in mind, the end in mind is Organizational High Performance. High performance organization is comprised of one or more teams, each consisting of two or more individuals, with all having complementary skills, interests, and beliefs brought together for coordinated activities to achieve a higher goal.

As presented earlier, the Fundamentals of Organizational High Performance consist of:

- The Management System
- The Business Model
- The Leadership Standard
- The Organizational Science
- The Organizational Action Research Schemata

Collectively these Fundamentals of Organizational High Performance provides the basics of driving your organization forward to achieving its desired future state.

Chapter 2:
The Management System

Introduction

An effective and efficient Management System is foundational to organizational high performance as it enables over the horizon planning by incorporating best practices to effectively lead and manage high-performing organizations. Applying the system to an organization ensures it has a clear procedural picture to develop or refine who they are, where they are going, and how they will get there from a transformational, collaborative, and integrative perspective. The system is structured around the best practices utilized to effectively lead and manage high-performance organizations.

A Management System is required to lead an organization effectively forward into the future. This integration is achieved by focusing on accomplishing these critical management tasks:

- Develop and communicate an organizational vision and mission
- Develop, communicate, and integrate strategic goals, objectives and performance measures
- Develop, communicate, assign, and implement business initiatives
- Obtain feedback and learn

As an overview, these critical tasks are recommended for any organization to truly move successfully forward.[16][17] These management tasks begin with establishing an organizational vision and mission. These goals, objectives, and performance measures then work to support the organization's vision and mission. The strategic objectives should achieve the organization's mission, vision, and strategy. The performance measures have both external and internal components. Externally, the performance measures focus on the organization's stakeholders and customers, while, internally, the performance measures focus on critical business processes, financials, innovation, and learning and growth. The business initiatives, when accomplished, will achieve the organization's goals and objectives. Lastly, one must adapt and learn through an established feedback mechanism.

The Management System enables an organization's enduring core functions to maintain their competitive advantage and unique value contributions to their stakeholders. Influenced by and acted on its surrounding environment, the

---

[16] Collins, J., & Porras, J. (1998). Organizational vision and visionary organizations. In G. R. Hickman (eds), *Leading organizations: Perspectives for a new era*, (pp. 234-249).

[17] Hart, S. (1992). An integrative framework for strategy-making processes. *The Academy of Management Review*, 17(2), 327-351.

System's strength lies in its utilization of five distinct, but interrelated management programs, which are:

- *Strategic Management*
- *Operations Management*
- *Resource Management*
- *Performance Management*
- *Communications Management*

The 360-degree perspective provided by the above mutually supporting and integrated programs provides numerous benefits. This system will result in a return on investment (ROI) in the form of increased organizational performance through the improvement of an organization's internal business processes as well as their business of access to their products, services, and expertise for the entire gamut of their stakeholders and customers.

Programs

The Management System (Figure 1) enables an organization to maintain their competitive advantage over other entities in their industry. To appreciate fully the strength of the Management System, one needs to understand its five distinct, but interrelated programs.

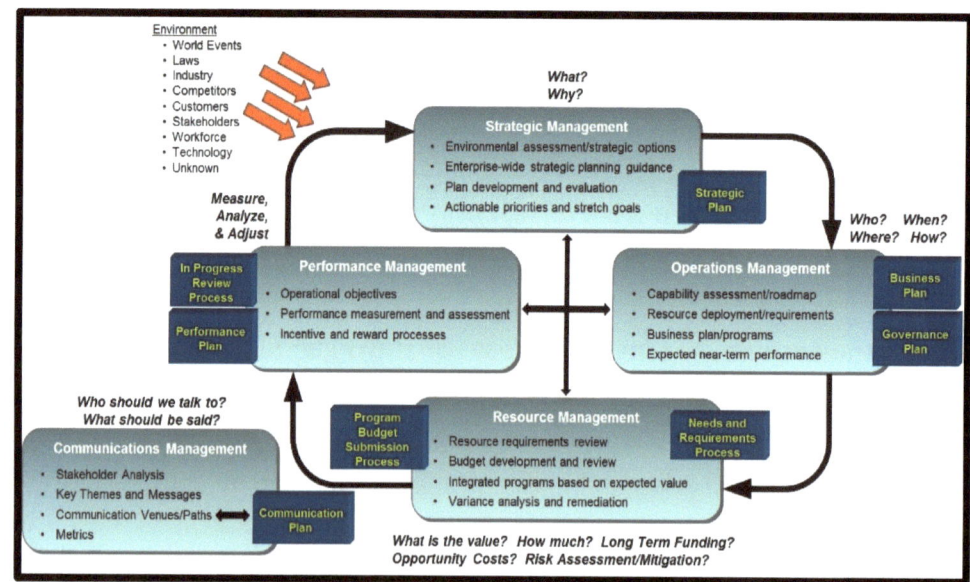

Figure 1: The Management System

Strategic Management

Strategic Management is the first step in implementing the Management System. An organization's strategic management develops and then translates their mission and vision into terms guiding real management decisions across the business units. It provides substantive direction to their business and guides management decision making.

The Strategic Management Program sets forth a definition of who an organization is, what they do, and why they do it. It establishes an Environmental assessment with strategic options. In assessing the environment, it is acknowledged an organization's stakeholders and customers have increasing needs for and desires access to the organization's products, services, expertise, and support. Additionally, the environment requires an increase in and a higher level of collaboration internal and external to the organization.

The Strategic Management Program provides guidance for an enterprise-wide strategic planning effort to set actionable goals, enabling objectives, and Business Initiatives examined through a Performance Management Program. This effort leverages an organization's core values, functions, and competencies. An organization's future *value proposition* is reliant upon a strategy with clearly articulated and comprehensive Goals and Enabling Objectives. To initiate the achievement of the Strategic Management Program, an organization should first identify key sources of value creation across the enterprise. From a general perspective, this involves defining an approach for achieving the goals and enabling objectives. This approach is then communicated through a Strategic Plan. From a specific perspective, typically, an organization develops its strategy at an annual two- or three-day offsite meeting. To begin, an organization should focus on its mission (purpose) and vision (aspiration for future results). Once affirming the mission and vision statements, an organization conducts a strategic analysis of their current operating environment. Several methodologies can be used to conduct this analysis such as:

- SWOT: Strengths, Weaknesses, Opportunities, and Threats
- PESTEL: Political, Economic, Social, Technological, Environment, and Legislative
- Porter's Five Forces:
    1. Threat of entry of new competitors
    2. The intensity of competitive rivalry
    3. The threat of substitute products or services
    4. The buying power of customers (buyers)
    5. The buying power of suppliers

Finally, an organization needs to determine how best to operate in this environment, and formulate a strategy with a series of goals and objectives. This activity establishes a foundation for the strategy and future stages of the framework.

Once the strategy is developed, an organization needs to translate it into actionable initiatives, which can be clearly communicated. One tool to do this is a strategy map, which helps visualize the cause-and-effect relationships among goals and objectives. For an organization, the map begins with the organization's mission and then links down to objectives for customer satisfaction, critical processes, and ultimately people and resources. Strategy maps can be developed at various levels, meaning an overall corporate strategy map can be broken down into functional strategy maps for different themes. One key element to the strategy map is balancing objectives across different perspectives. The aforementioned customer, process, people, and resource perspectives are typically used for an organization. A strategy map can be simplified by breaking it into several strategic themes. A strategic theme, typically a vertical slice within the map, consists of a distinct set of related strategic objectives. One benefit of these vertical strategic themes is they deliver results over periods of time, based on the cause and effect relationships of the objectives. From the strategy map, an organization can choose to use another tool, such as a balanced scorecard, to identify strategic performance targets. These are linked to the objectives within the strategy map, and are often used as the basis for selecting initiatives in the next stage.

Operations Management

The Operations Management Program provides information as to who, when, where, and how the activity will be accomplishing an organization's mission as well as its Business Initiatives. The Operations Management Program lays out a series of tactical or near-time enabling objectives and business initiatives for an organization, as they are its operational entities. It is in essence the Roadmap, Business Plan, and Governance Plan to enable the Business Initiative Leads to achieve their endeavors. It includes deploying resources based upon existing requirements.

The four components of the Management System are equal in importance; however, it must be recognized organizational operations are the key element with all of the other endeavors in supportive roles. No component can survive without the other component. Therefore, the Operations Management Program is the execution arm of the directorate's Strategic Plan with interaction with the Performance and Resource Management Programs. Operations Management sets the investment priorities for executing the business strategy. These priorities are monitored, analyzed, and adapted through the Performance Management Program. The Operations Management Program sets the stage for an activity based on the integration with the other three programs to achieve a portfolio of business initiatives aligned to strategic themes, goals, and enabling objectives.

Based on these developed strategic themes, goals, and enabling objectives, an organization should launch initiatives with action plans to enable the targets to be achieved. An initiative is a discretionary program or project of finite duration designed to close some type of gap. Initiatives must be viewed as an integrated bundle of investments, as opposed to stand-alone projects, and ideally should be selected so they link to a strategic theme. By doing so, organizations will benefit from the integrated impact of initiatives aligned to multiple objectives. Organizations will get the largest return of their investment by focusing on initiatives directly related to objectives concurrently aligned with long-term strategic goals and themes. Typically, an operation plan (business plan and roadmap) comprises a series of these initiatives. As part of this plan, an organization should also determine the resources required to execute the initiatives. One tool to accomplish this determination is activity-based costing (ABC).

Resource Management

The Resource Management Program is a set of processes for choosing among competing priorities and control mechanisms for holding areas to specific investment levels. It provides a common comprehensive fiscal picture as well as enables meaningful quantitative trade studies and scenario analyses. Additionally, the Resource Management Program provides answers to such questions as, what is the value; how much; opportunity costs; risk assessment/mitigation; and long term funding. The process which answers these questions includes: Resource Requirements Reviews, Budget Development and Reviews, Variance Analysis and Remediation, and Program Integration based on expected value. During the process activity, resource assessments determine how under or over investments are planned for and conducted as well as capture the synergies across an organization.

The budget should be linked to an organization's Strategic Management Program's activities as well as the Strategic Goals, Enabling Objectives, and individual Business Initiatives. It is critical to set budgets at the right level of granularity as overly detailed budgets result in micro management and produce the wrong incentives. The budget processes must remain flexible enough to respond to any major discontinuities. Budgeting controls should reinforce performance management processes to send consistent signals and in place for understanding variances. Therefore, the budget needs only to be detailed enough to permit adequate execution with reporting processes at a periodicity to permit adjustments to be made with the necessary lead-time as to not affect operations.

Performance Management

Performance management aligns an organization behind a common business strategy and provides visibility into its performance via metrics. It translates the strategy into operationally meaningful objectives and tracks performance against those objectives. A mature Performance Management Program will inform decisions on an organization's many endeavors, culminating in well-documented corporate memory that can identify longer-term trends and patterns. The data collected through this Performance Management Program will provide insight into how efficiently and effectively an organization is accomplishing its mission. It includes a mechanism for interpreting metrics and acting on the resulting data to enable corrective actions. Therefore, the Performance Management Program can highlight potential deficiencies or strengths across an organization and enable harmonization and best practice transfer. The activity within the program set forth a clear view of what an organization believes is important and sets for a management style based upon performance. A Performance Management Program creates an approach for defining, interpreting and guiding operational performance.

The Performance Management Program within an organization should be conducted efficiently throughout the organization leading to consistent data reporting to internal and external decision-making bodies. Through a centralized Performance Management Program, an organization will be able to gather performance data once and report it many times from different points of view. Effective execution requires the establishment and tracking of quantifiable metrics to determine the degree of progress made to accomplish an organization's mission, vision, strategic goals, and enabling objectives (i.e., results oriented management). An integrated performance process is critical to create accountability for performance outcomes that best reflect the mission, priorities, and goals of an organization. Performance management is a critical step in ensuring results and successes are identified and measured for any program or project and manages investments where value often is difficult to capture. Performance management can have both immediate and far-reaching impacts on an organization and brings with it an emphasis on objectivity, fairness, consistency, and responsiveness. At the same time, performance management functions as a reliable indicator of an organization's long-term health. Other benefits include:

- **Ownership and interdepartmental collaboration** - By providing clear direction for efforts in a particular functional area, performance measurement gives employees a greater investment in problem solving, goal setting, and process improvements. It helps set priorities and promotes collaboration among the organization.
- **Communication and a common language** - Reporting results can enhance staff, stakeholder, and partner understanding and support of strategies and decisions. The reporting process provides a common language, raises awareness of potential problem areas, and encourages inter-organization knowledge sharing.
- **Accountability** - Well-designed performance measures document progress towards achievement of goals and objectives, motivating and catalyzing organizations to fulfill their obligations to their employees, clients, stakeholders, partners, customers, and investors.

- **Budget justification** - Performance measurement ties activities to results and, therefore, is a long-term planning tool that can justify resource allocation.

There are three components within the Performance Management Program: Monitor, Analyze, and Adapt. The leadership team of the organization must also meet periodically to monitor the progress of its strategy. This monitoring could occur quarterly or annually. This monitoring activity will obtain data used to assess the strategic environment from a holistic perspective as well as how each strategic theme, goal, enabling objective, and individual business initiative is progressing. An organization needs to hold regular meetings on the same periodicity as the data collection to analyze the data related to the execution of their strategic and operational plans. A management board of senior leaders may hold a review less frequently, but still must monitor and assess the overall performance of the organization. An organization should meet frequently to review performance dashboards and address short-term issues. Performance based dashboards are based on the organization's critical processes and operation plan and the use of data collection tools, such as surveys and web-crawlers. An organization's leadership should come prepared to discuss the performance results, gaps in performance, and any issues at these performance reviews. Rather than spending the meeting listening to performance reports for the first time, mangers should spend the meeting discussing the issues, implications, and devising plans to address the issues. These operational performance reviews can be held at various or multiple levels within the organization. An organization leader may want to hold their own review of a particular area. If during the strategic monitoring, an organization discovers there are issues in one of these areas, adjustments can be made as necessary and adapt to the issues. This adaptation could mean making incremental changes or completely revamping the area of contention.

The Performance Management program identifies three performance areas: Stakeholder/Customer Satisfaction, Quality Assurance, and Workforce Strength. These performance areas will enable an organization to determine their overall success.

- **Stakeholder/Customer Satisfaction**: Meeting or exceeding the organizational stakeholder and customer needs by helping them achieve their mission outcomes and business goals; delivering value to stakeholders and customers. Stakeholder/customer satisfaction is increased through:
    - Timeliness: Ability to respond within requested timeframes.
    - Relevance: The usefulness of an organization's products, services, and expertise.

- o Accuracy: The extent to which an organization's products, services, and expertise are reliable.
- o Accessibility: The organizational stakeholders and customers' ability to discover relevant products, services, and expertise.
- o Impact: Ability of the organization to meet or exceed their stakeholders' and customers' needs.
- **Quality Assurance**: Ensuring the stakeholders and customers have the most valid and useful products, services, and expertise so to achieve their mission outcomes and business goals. Quality assurance is increased through:
  - o Research: The processes an organization uses to identify product, service, and expertise gaps.
  - o Collaboration: The processes an organization uses to share information across the organization so to develop and present the best products, services, and expertise to its stakeholders and customers.
  - o Analysis and Production: The processes an organization uses to address stakeholder and customer needs.
  - o Quality Reviews: The processes an organization uses to inject rigor into the development of its products, services, and expertise.
  - o Dissemination: The processes an organization uses to ensure its products, services, and expertise are discoverable.
- **Workforce Strength**: Recruiting, retaining, and developing a capable workforce prepared to deliver products, services, and expertise through which to address evolving stakeholder and customer needs. The strength of the workforce is increased through:
  - o Workforce Stability: The degree to which an organization experiences changes in the workforce supply due to turnover and/or potential for turnover.
  - o Proficiency: The degree to which the workforce is adequately skilled and able to master new skills as needed.
  - o Experience Mix: The degree to which the depth of skill, tenure mix, and distribution of experience meets an organization's needs.
  - o Alignment: The extent to which an organization's workforce is appropriately arrayed against its mission and business goals.
  - o Employee Climate: Workforce perceptions of an organization's work environment.

Focusing on these performance areas will enable an organization's leadership to evaluate the true impact that it has on its stakeholders and customers.

Communications Management

Perhaps the single most important tool facilitating the movement of people and an organization forward is communication. Many efforts fail due to ineffective communication activities but effective communication can be linked to the implementation of successful change efforts.

Communication is, in general, the exchange of thoughts, messages, or information. Effective communications is the process of enabling two-way information sharing, which allows the receiving party to understand easily the message sent by another party. To be an effective communicator and to get the point across without misunderstanding and confusion, the goal should be to lessen the frequency of these barriers at each stage of this process with clear, concise, accurate, well-planned communications.

An effective communication process begins with a sender who encodes a message within a particular context and passes it through some channel to the receiver who decodes accurately the message with an understanding of the same context then provides feedback to ensure the message and context received is the same that was transmitted. Graphically, the process is depicted in Figure 2.

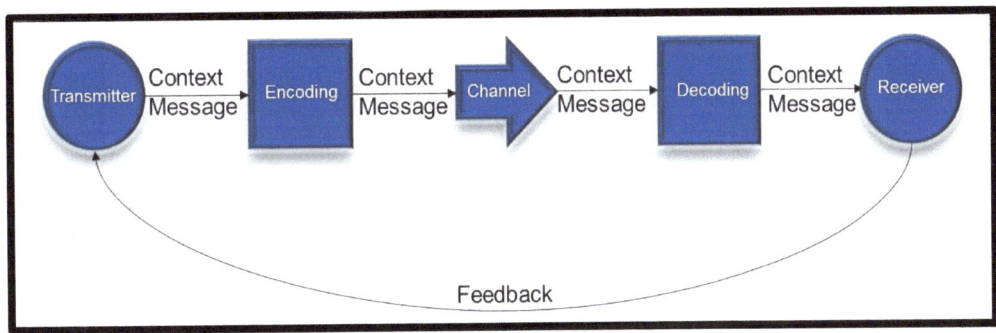

Figure 2: Communication Process

The communication process is comprised of seven components. These components are:

- **Transmitter**: As the source of the message, you need to be clear about why you are communicating, and what you want to communicate. You also need to be confident that the information you are communicating is useful and accurate.
- **Context**: The situation in which your message is delivered is the context. This may include the surrounding environment or broader culture (corporate culture, international cultures, and so on).
- **Message**: The message is the information you want to communicate.
- **Encoding**: This is the process of transferring the information you want to communicate into a form that can be sent and correctly decoded at

the other end. Your success in encoding depends partly on your ability to convey information clearly and simply, but also on your ability to anticipate and eliminate sources of confusion (for example, cultural issues, mistaken assumptions, and missing information.). A key part of this is knowing your audience: Failure to understand who you are communicating with will result in delivering messages that are misunderstood.

- **Channel**: Messages are conveyed through channels, with verbal including face-to-face meetings, telephone and videoconferencing; and written including letters, text based electronic communications, memos, and reports. Different channels have different strengths and weaknesses. For example, it is not particularly effective to give a long list of directions verbally, while you will quickly cause problems if you criticize someone strongly by email.

- **Decoding**: Just as successful encoding is a skill, so is successful decoding (involving, for example, taking the time to read a message carefully, or listen actively to it.). Just as confusion can arise from errors in encoding, it can also arise from decoding errors. This is particularly the case if the decoder does not have enough knowledge to understand the message.

- **Receiver**: Message are delivered to individual members of your audience. No doubt, you have in mind the actions or reactions you hope your message will get from this audience. Keep in mind, though, that each of these individuals enters into the communication process with ideas and feelings that will undoubtedly influence their understanding of your message, and their response. To be a successful communicator, you should consider these before delivering your message, and act appropriately.

- **Feedback**: Your audience will provide you with feedback, verbal and nonverbal reactions to your communicated message. Pay close attention to this feedback, as it is the only thing that allows you to be confident that your audience has understood your message. If you find that there has been a misunderstanding, at least you have the opportunity to send the message a second time.

There are numerous techniques, known as the seven C's, through which to increase the propensity for effective communications. These seven Cs are:

- **Completeness:** The communication must be complete. It should convey all facts required by the audience. The sender of the message must take into consideration the receiver's mindset and convey the

message accordingly. Complete communication has the following features:
- Develops and enhances the reputation of an organization.
- Is cost saving, as no crucial information is missing and no additional cost is incurred by needing to convey extra messages.
- Gives additional information wherever required and eaves no questions in the mind of receiver.
- Helps in better decision-making by the audience/readers/receivers of message as they get all desired and crucial information.
- Persuades the audience.

- **Conciseness:** Conciseness means wordiness, i.e., communicating what you want to convey in least possible words without forgoing the other C's of communication. Conciseness is a necessity for effective communication. Concise communication has following features:
  - Is both time- and cost-saving.
  - Underlines and highlights the main message, as it avoids using excessive and needless words.
  - Provides short and essential message in limited words to the audience.
  - Is more appealing and comprehensible to the audience.
  - Is non-repetitive in nature.

- **Consideration:** Consideration implies "stepping into the shoes of others". Effective communication must take the audience into consideration, i.e., the audience's viewpoints, background, mind-set, and education level. Make an attempt to envision our audience, their requirements, emotions as well as problems. Ensure that the self-respect of the audience is maintained and their emotions are not at harm. Modify your words and message to suit the audience's needs while making your message complete. Features of considerate communication are as follows:
  - Emphasize on "you" approach.
  - Empathize with the audience and exhibit interest in the audience. This will stimulate a positive reaction from the audience.
  - Show optimism towards your audience. Emphasize on "what is possible" rather than "what is impossible". Lay stress on positive words such as jovial, committed, thanks, warm, healthy, and help.

- **Clarity:** Clarity implies emphasizing on a specific message or goal at a time, rather than trying to achieve too much at once. Clarity in communication has the following features:

- o Enables easier understanding.
- o Enhances the message's meaning.
- o Makes use of exact, appropriate, and concrete words.
- **Concreteness:** Concrete communication implies being particular and clear rather than fuzzy and general. Concreteness strengthens the confidence. A Concrete message has the following features:
    - o Supports with specific data.
    - o Uses words that are clear and that build the reputation.
    - o Makes understanding easy.
- **Courtesy:** Courtesy in a message implies the message should show the sender's expression as well as their respect of the receiver. The sender of the message should be sincerely polite, judicious, reflective and enthusiastic. Courteous messages have the following features:
    - o Takes into consideration both viewpoints as well as feelings of the receiver of the message.
    - o Is positive and focused at the audience.
    - o Makes use of terms showing respect for the receiver of message.
    - o Is unbiased.
- **Correctness:** Correctness in communication implies there are no grammatical errors. Correct communication has the following features:
    - o Provides an exact and well-timed message.
    - o Boosts the receiver's confidence level.
    - o Enables a greater impact on the audience/readers.
    - o Checks for the precision and accurateness of data used in the message.
    - o Makes use of appropriate and correct language in the message.

The essence of communications management is the systematic and purposeful process of engaging with an audience. Engaging implies communications is a two-way process. Communications management, to claim the two-process is successful, must address:[18]

- What information needs to flow?
- Who needs what information?
- When will the information be required?
- In what format and by which channel will the information be provided?
- Who will be responsible for ensuring the information is provided?
- How will the communications' effectiveness be measured?

---

[18] PMHut.com (n.d.). Retrieved on August 23, 2016, from http://www.pmhut.com/communication-and-collaboration-in-project-management-introduction

A Communication Management Plan is an enabler to any endeavor. It lets people know where they are going, why they are going, and how they plan to get there. Its objectives are to:

- Identify and provide an evaluation on the stakeholders
- Identify in what grouping the stakeholder belongs to (champion or resistor)
- Identify the communication needs of the stakeholder groups
- Identify and provide consistent, relevant, accurate, and applicable messages to each stakeholder group
- Minimize the spread of miscommunication
- Build stakeholder ownership, commitment, and readiness toward the endeavor
- Identify and implement measures to assess the Communication Management Plan's effectiveness

Conclusion

This Management System focuses on an organization and its core functions. It utilizes a 360-degree perspective through mutually supporting and integrating programs in order to be implemented and executed successfully. This system will result in a return on investment (ROI) by increasing organizational performance through the improvement of its internal business processes as well as their business of providing products, services, and expertise for its stakeholders and customers.

The Strategic Management Program focuses the organization's leadership and workforce. It explicitly dictates what the organization wants to achieve and why these goals and enabling objectives are important. The Operations Management Program sets forth the business initiatives necessary to accomplish the Strategic Plan. It indicates who, where, when, and how the business initiatives are achieved. The Resource Management Program is responsible for allocating resources toward business initiatives. The Performance Management Program will measure the business initiative to determine how well it is progressing as well as to indicate when it has come to fruition. Additionally, this program will collect, analyze and integrate data from across the organization and enhance the flow of information. By focusing on mission-oriented performance metrics, an organization's leadership can better demonstrate the impact of management and resource decisions.

An organization can succeed in enabling the information-age technology by investing and managing their intellectual assets. Specialization of functionality should be integrated with a customer-focused paradigm. Flexibility, responsiveness, and high quality products, services, and expertise delivered via innovative use of technology will move an organization forward to a future-state of better business. Lastly, these success concepts in the information-age must be captured with mission and vision statements inspiring and bonding the workforce of the organization by being able to focus the knowledge, skills, and abilities of the workforce to achieve an organization's strategic vision and mission as well as its business goals and objectives. The way ahead beyond the acceptance and adoption of this Management System is to use it as a springboard to move forward by implementing or maturing each of the programs.

Chapter 3:
The Business Model

Introduction

An appropriate business model is foundational to organizational high performance. In today's arduous environment, organizations must adapt, overcome, and improvise to meet quickly and efficiently the pressures and demands of a modern environment. As James Duderstadt said, "We face a future in which permanence and stability become less important than flexibility and creativity, in which one of the few certainties will be the presence of continual change."[19] Organizations must rely on the knowledge, skills, and experience of a wide range of people to solve multifaceted problems, make good decisions, and deliver effective solutions to achieve successfully their strategic vision. The business model detailed next (Figure 3) illustrates the dynamics of organizational development through the synthesis of various models. Leveraging accurately the concepts of this business model will deliver significant results by developing a high performance organization capable of collaboratively increasing teamwork, customer satisfaction, and mission accomplishment.

The Business Model

Besides having an understanding of what is a high performance organization, organizational leaders must utilize a holistic business model through which to know the components of an organization (Figure 3). This understanding is important because the model provides the areas in which to focus on when an organization is moving toward high performance. All organizations have these components; however, their quality and level is what determines the difference between mediocre or high performance organizations.

Just knowing the components is not enough; an organization must understand how they contribute to creating a high performance organization.[20]

---

[19] Duderstadt, J. (2000; p35). *A university for the 21st century*. Ann Arbor, MI: University of Michigan Press.

[20] Lawler, E., Mohrman, S. A., & Benson, G. S. (2001). Organizing for high performance: The CEO report on employee involvement, TQM, reengineering, and knowledge management in fortune 1000 companies. San Francisco, CA: Jossey-Bass.

To start a review of the Business Model for high performance organizations (Figure 3), one should begin at the heart of the organization, which is the Core Goals and Values, then start developing the strategy and move through the model in a clockwise direction. All of the components of an organization are developed within the context of its environment.

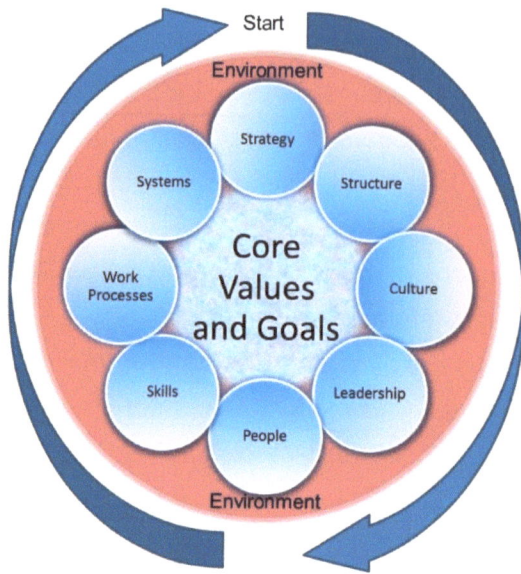

Figure 3: Business Model

Core Values and Goals

Definition: Fundamental ideas, guiding concepts, values and aspirations, sometimes unwritten, beyond formal statements of corporate objectives

Information: The organization's mission and vision should be the foundation of the organization but they are associated with core values and goals. An organization's core values and goals are the background on which all components are aligned to achieve organizational high performance. The efficiency and accuracy the core values and goals are transmitted, understood, and the organizational components are aligned with them throughout the company correlates to the Profit/Loss margin.[21]

Strategy

Definition: It is the governance documents stating how an organization will attain its vision. It is comprised of its Strategic, Business, Communications, and Performance Management Plan.

Information: *If one does not know where they are going, then any road will do; the un-aimed arrow never misses its target.* This logic does not promote the

---

[21] Baum, J., Locke, L., & Kirkpactrick, S. (1998). A longitudinal study of the relation of vision and vision communication to venture growth in entrepreneurial firms. *Journal of Applied Psychology*, 83(1), 43-54.

likelihood of achieving a successful outcome. Successful outcomes are achieved primarily through thoughtful and purposeful planning. For an organization to achieve high performance, it must first determine where it wants to go, how it is going to get there, and have a designated timeline with checkpoints and milestones. A Business Plan must align with a Strategic Plan, which is focused on the organizational core goals, values, mission, and vision.

Structure

Definition: The characteristics and forms of how people are organized in relation to each other and to the work flow.

Information: An appropriate organizational structure promotes clarity of alignment to the holistic organization, the efficiency of communications, and everyone's roles and responsibilities. A high performance organizational structure is one in which the whole organization understands, agrees with, and trusts it.

Culture

Definition: The organizational norms as reflected in people's behavior and language, the product of group experience, and the style of leadership in an organization.

Information: An organizational culture just does not instantaneously exist. It evolves over time and is continuously dynamic and ever changing and influenced by positive and negative reinforcement. Just as every individual is unique and different though similar to other individuals so is the culture of an organization. An organizational culture promotes and sustains a work environment. How well or how poorly the work environment creates and sustains a high performance organization is determined by outcomes. Cultures promoting high performance organizations will utilize their industry's best practices as defined as those activities resulting in the highest levels of outcomes for the organization and their stakeholders. As an organization's culture is comprised of people, human capital, Human Resource (HR) is paramount to developing the desired organizational culture supportive of high performance.

Research has explored the correlation between culture and high performance organizations. A culture promoting respect, shared goals and values, teamwork, and creating an internal work environment whereas the organizational human capital work collaboratively towards achieving the organizational mission, vision, and strategic goals contributes to the organizational success and subsequently it being determined as high performing. A culture focused on innovation and customer satisfaction creates a work environment most beneficial to supporting a high performance organization.[22] Additionally, the more senior leaders are involved in and aware of the organizational culture, the higher the propensity of the existence of a high performance organization, implying senior leaders should drive the organizational culture. The absence of senior leaders' involvement in communication, planning, and promoting the organizational culture, the lower the likelihood of organizational high performance.

Leadership

Definition: How the senior leaders behave through invested time, attention, and symbolic actions.

Information: High performance organizations have senior leaders with a firm grasp of the capabilities and services offered by their organization's business units as well as the markets in which the business units operate. They also know how business units support the organizational mission and vision. This knowledge enables the creation of appropriate strategy to move forward to achieve goals and objectives leading to mission success.

The organizational leaders should be innovative, constantly renewing and creating, and always on the leading edge. Leaders in high performance organizations:

- model and mentor the desired behaviors
- provide a Vision/Mission/Philosophy
- use situational based leadership
- delegate authority and empower human capital in the decision making process
- ensure clear expectations
- promote a sense of urgency
- speak regularly about performance

People (Human Capital)

Definition: The individuals in the organization, the corporate demographics. It is not individual personalities.

Information: People, human capital, provide a high performance organization with the competitive advantage over its competitors. Organizational high performance human capital is engaged in daily operations of the business with the necessary knowledge, skills, and motivation as well as in the growth of the business.[23] It is the HR Department's recruitment activities in an organization

---

[22] HayGroup. (2005, February). *What makes the most admired companies great?* Retrieved January 17, 2008, from http://www.haygroup.com

[23] Hewitt, A. (2007). *Building a high-performance workforce.* Retrieved April 3, 2012, from http://www.hewittassociates.com

driving the attainment of a high performance workforce. Indeed, high performance organizations ranked the activities of high performance employees as a critical cog in improving an organizational bottom line.[24] Therefore, largely, the HR department is responsible for the organizational high performance.[25]

Skills

Definition: The organizational capabilities as a whole as opposed to just the capabilities of its employees.

Information: Skills have both an organizational and individual aspect. Skills do not only mean the individual employees' ability to perform their job description. It also means the organization's ability to achieve its strategic goals and extrapolate them to achieve business objectives. Both aspects must utilize and promote the cognitions, behaviors, and emotions desired to achieve the ultimate end state of high performance. There are many individual and organizational skills; however, the valid skills should complement the organizational mission and vision and promoting high performance through a highly effective work environment, which encompasses the whole organization.

Work Processes

Definition: A major set of interconnected activities organized in time through which inputs are used, deliverables are produced, and customer feedback is used to make improvements.

Information: The organizational processes should be supportive and aligned with the core goals and values to achieve the activities' objectives. Will the processes get the organization to their desired mission of high performance? Processes, working optimally, will increase efficiencies, increase productivity, and improve profit margins. Processes misaligned with the organizations core goals, values, and strategic direction result in a poor performance management program because the wrong metrics are used to determine success.

As an example of an effective process, organizational human capital developed through effective HR recruitment practices should be aligned with the organization's mission, vision and overarching Strategic Plan.[26] This straight forward and some may say obvious statement is not practiced in all organizations to the

---

[24] Balaguer, E., Cheese, P., & Marchetti, C. (2006). *The high performance workforce study*. Retrieved January 10, 2008, from http://www.accenture.com

[25] Ulrich, D., & Brockbank, W. (2005). *The HR value proposition*. Boston, MA: Harvard Business School Press

[26] Liu, Y., Combs, J., Ketchen, D., & Ireland, R. (2007). The value of human resource management for organizational performance. *Business Horizons, 50*(6), 503-511.

degree it should. The integration and alignment of processes to strategy has been determined to be a value added resulting in increased revenue.[27]

Human capital processes include: Competency Management, Career Development, Performance Appraisal, Succession Planning, Recruiting, Workforce Planning, Workplace Design, Rewards and Recognition, Employee Relations, Human Capital Strategy, Learning Management, Knowledge Management, Human Capital Infrastructure.[28]

Systems

Definition: The coherent set of actions aimed at gaining a sustainable advantage over competition.

Information: Creating a Management System enables over the horizon planning by incorporating best practices to effectively lead and manage high-performing organizations.[29] Such a system moves the organization toward the future to create a set of processes and procedures developing and refining the organization as well as determining where it is going and how it will get there from a transformational, collaborative, and integrative perspective.

A Management System enables a high performance organization's enduring core goals and values to maintain their competitive advantage and contribute to its bottom line. The System's strength lies in its utilization of five distinct, but mutually supporting and interrelated management programs:

- Strategic Management
- Operations Management
- Resource Management
- Performance Management
- Communications Management

The above management program provides numerous benefits. This system will result in a return on investment in the form of increased organizational performance through the improvement of the organizational internal business processes as well as their Profit/Loss margin. Systems, like processes, must be congruent with the organizational core goals, values, and strategic direction to ensure the achievement of organizational high performance.

---

[27] Combs, J., Liu, Y., Hall, A., Ketchen, D. (2006). How much do high-performance work practices matter? A meta-analysis of their effects on organizational performance. *Personnel Psychology*, 59(3), 501-528.

[28] Cantrell, S., Benton, M., Laudal, T., & Thomas, R. (2006). Measuring the value of human capital investments: The SAP case. *Strategy & Leadership*, 34(2), 43-52.

[29] Kaplan, R., & Norton, D. (2007, July/August). Using the balanced scorecard as a strategic management tool. *Harvard Business Review*. (Reprinted from *Harvard Business Review*, January/February 1996).

Environment

Definition: The holistic dynamic atmosphere comprised of the internal and external forces influencing the organization's return on investment.

Information: The environment has both internal and external forces that puts stress and tension on the organization. As mentioned above, the influence these forces have on an organization and its ability to be high performing is measured by how well the strategic goals and objectives are achieved. There is a positive correlation between an organization's internal work environment and its recruitment and retention levels. In addition, the research indicates a positive correlation between an organization's internal work environment and its employee's motivation, sense of belonging, and the development of a high performance organization.[30]

The external environmental force is extremely influential to an organization. The organization's stakeholders, customers, suppliers, and the public comprise the external environment. Assessing these forces perception on the organization's performance can provide critical insight into the organization's ability to meet its mission, vision and strategic goals. This measurement of the external forces is a reflection of the organization's performance and behaviors. As an example of how strong the external environment can be, let us use customers. Customers want the most product and service for their money. This point equates to high value, speed to produce, quality assurance levels, and innovative solutions. Customers are definitely not supportive of poor performance, which diminishes their loyalty level. If their needs are not being met, customers will leave and go to an organization's competitors.

Conclusion

Regardless of the organization, it is a function of its leader. As the leader is, so will be the organization. Therefore, the choice of who will be the leader is a critical component of the organization's success. The leader must choose the methodology with which to develop a high performance organization. There are multiple paths on which to achieve high performance. Kotter's eight-phase approach is one path that works well to develop organizations with a shared vision, senior management commitment, direction, involvement, communication and processes as well as other attributes of high performance.[31] Using Lewin's methodology,[32] which was

---

[30] Colvin, G. (2007, October). How top companies breed stars. *Fortune Magazine*. Retrieved January 10, 2008, from http://www.fortune.com

[31] Kotter, J. (1995). Leading change: Why transformation efforts fail. *Harvard Business Review* (March-April, 1995).

[32] Lewin, K. (1947). Frontiers in-group dynamics: Concept, method, and reality in social science; social equilibria, and social change. *Human Relations*, 1(1), 5-41.

confirmed by Moran and Brightman,[33] to handle change management issues complements this approach. No matter what path is chosen, the characteristics of high performance organizations and thus what we strive to achieve are:

- Leadership
- The team shares common goals
- Explicit and shared values supported by a clear value system
- Members know their individual roles
- Pride, openness, trust, honesty, motivation, enthusiasm and respect for individuals
- Atmosphere is informal with information transparent to all team members
- Everyone is included in discussions
- Conflict is not avoided but used to identify team issues
- Pride in the team and team performance

These characteristics are in general agreement with Oakland whereby the organization is committed because the employees have participated in generating ideas and selecting alternatives, and they have a role to play in the work as well as the evaluation of the work when it is finished.[34] This atmosphere is conducive to improvements in learning and development as well as in motivation and commitment on the organization's behalf. It is also an ideal needing to be sought after if the teamwork is to continue to improve the morale within an organization and achieve organizational goals and objectives. The key enablers of a high performance organization are:

- Individual employees' competencies
- Skills, processes, tools, and techniques
- Interpersonal skills, communications, and personality preferences
- Value systems
- Shared vision, purpose, goals, direction
- Organizational values including openness
- Intelligence, knowledge and experience
- Creativity, flexibility, adaptability, willingness to try new ideas, concepts, and processes
- Courage and willingness to take risks
- Mutual support and help

---

[33] Moran, J., & Brightman, B. (2000). Leading organizational change. *Journal of Workplace Learning: Employee Counseling Today*, 12(2), 66-74.

[34] Oakland, J. (1995). *Total quality management.* (2nd ed.). Waltham, MA: Butterworth Heinemann.

These enablers are similar to the results of Hastings, Bixby, and Chaudry-Lawton, who devised a list of *Ten Golden Rules* for successfully working in high performance organizations.[35]

In conclusion, the business model adapts extremely well for the demands of the modern business environment. When using it in any environment think about the aspects of performance necessary for success in the situation and incorporate local relevant factors into the model to create a specific interpretation. A very useful organizational framework will result leading toward organizational high performance.

---

[35] Hastings, C., Bixby, P., & Chaudry-Lawton, R. (1986). *Super teams – Building organizational success through high-performing teams*. Englewood Cliffs, NJ: Prentice Hall International.

This page left blank intentionally.

Chapter 4:
The Leadership Standard

Introduction

Leadership is the process of influencing people by providing purpose, direction, and motivation to accomplish the mission and improve the organization.[36] Management is the process of dealing with or controlling things or people.[37] Leaders and managers play different roles in organizations.[38] Leaders seek to change organizations, while managers sustain and control them. Invariably intertwined with leadership is management and vice versa; therefore, for the sake of discussion, though understanding they are different, the term leadership and being a leader will encapsulate both concepts.

The challenge of leadership is there are numerous leadership theories and paradigms through which the processes of influencing and dealing with people are implemented.[39] Of course, they are considered valid by their developer. Some of these leadership theories and paradigms include:

- autocratic, democratic, or laissez faire
- bottom-up or top-down
- centralized or decentralized
- customer-, product-, or service-oriented
- servant, situational, participative, or transformational

One must realize the concept of leadership is not static since it is constantly influenced both by internal dynamics of organizations and by the external environment. A high performance leader has the following skills: (i) listen more than talk, (ii) cooperate more than compete; (iii) value talent more than title; (iv) value teamwork more than individual glory; (v) pursue purpose beyond profit; (vi) fix things not broken; (vii) take appropriate risks; generate new ideas; (vii) embrace change. Moreover, effective leadership requires a focus on values, assumptions, believes, and expectations (VABEs) at the organizational level.[40]

---

[36] Headquarters, Department of the Army (2012). *ADP 6-22: Army leadership*. Washington, D.C.: Department of the Army. Retrieved on May 23, 2016, from http://armypubs.army.mil/doctrine/DR_pubs/dr_a/pdf/adp6_22.pdf

[37] Oxford University Press (2016). Management: Definition. Retrieved on May 23, 2016, from http://www.oxforddictionaries.com/us/definition/american_english/management

[38] Beckhard, R., & Pritchard, W. (1992). Changing the essence: The art of creating and leading fundamental change in organizations. San Francisco, CA: Jossey-Bass.

[39] Legacee Academy (n.d.). Types of leadership styles. Retrieved on May 23, 2016, form https://www.legacee.com/types-of-leadership-styles/

[40] Kirkpatrick, S., & Locke, A. (1991). Leadership: Do traits matter? *Academy of Management Executive,* 5(2), 48-60.

If one researches the various leadership theories and paradigms as well as takes into account the numerous skills of high performance leaders, then there are a limited number of valid leadership styles. These styles center on:

- **Servant Leadership:** Analogous of, or can be said to focus on the environment, enabling people, and change. It is the foundation upon which all other leadership styles rest because it focus on enabling the workforce to achieve results.
- **Environmental Leadership:** Analogous of, or can be said to focus on the forces at play internal and external to the organization. The organizational environment, both internal and external, comprises of pressures and forces affecting and influencing the organization.
- **Participative Leadership:** Analogous of, or can be said to focus on driving change within or internal to the organization. All leadership is about adapting to or changing because of the environmental pressures and forces.
- **Situational Leadership:** Analogous of, or can be said to focus on the workforce. People are the hub of leadership because people are the center of all organizational activities.

When these leadership styles are collectively utilized, they meet the particular situational demands, the particular requirements of the people involved, and the particular organizational challenges during change. Therefore, these leadership styles are the main four upon which organizational high performance is based.

Leadership
Defined

Individual leadership is "influencing people by providing purpose, direction, and motivation while operating to accomplish the mission and improve the organization."[41] Effective leadership equates to effective team building.[42] An organization working together as one team, in-step and striving effectively toward commonly held goals, is foundational to organizational high performance. Therefore, the leader's ability to accomplish more from the employees, as a collective, than the sum of the employee's individual accomplishments is what defines the top management/supervisor leadership.[43]

---

[41] Department of the Army (1999). *Field manual 22-100: Army leadership -- Be, know, do*. Washington, DC: Department of the Army.

[42] Maddux, B., & Wingfield, B. (2003). *Team building: An exercise in leadership* (4th ed.). Menlo Park, CA: Crisp.

[43] Doren, D., McCutcheon, A., Evans, M., MacMillan, K., Hall, L., Pringle, D., et al. (September, 2004). Impact of the manager's span of control on leadership and performance. *Canadian*

Types and Levels

There are, in essence, two types of leadership: Indirect and Direct. The difference between the two levels is the type of interaction a leader has with their workforce. The indirect type of leadership is sub-divided into two leadership levels, which are strategic and organizational, and works at achieving results through leading, coaching, and mentoring direct leaders. The direct type of leadership is its own level of leadership and works at the immediate contact with the workforce.

Joseph Jaworski's Synchronicity Principles indicate, "Because of our obsessions with how leaders behave and with the interactions of leaders and followers, we forget that in its essence, leadership is about learning how to shape the future. Leadership exists when people are no longer victims of circumstances but participate in creating new circumstances. When people operate in this domain of generative leadership, day by day, they come to a deepening understanding of 'how the universe actually works'. That is the real gift of leadership. It is not about positional power; it is not about accomplishments; it is ultimately not even about what we do. Leadership is about creating a domain in which human beings continually deepen their understanding of reality and become more capable of participating in the unfolding of the world. Ultimately, leadership is about creating new realities."[44]

Leadership is about innovation and changing the status quo. Leadership, from a Gestalt perspective, is about creating a team whereas the whole achieves more collectively than the sum of the team's individual components. As noted, there are subsequently three leadership levels. The military, specifically the U.S. Army, indicates the three levels of leadership are:[45]

- **Strategic**: Strategic leaders must influence an organization of organizations and teams, which are possibly geographically dispersed. These leaders have limited direct contact with most organizational members. Because of their understanding of the holistic work environment, strategic leaders are focused on the bigger picture as they set the strategic direction of the entire organization, which are aligned with collaboration and unity of mission. They evaluate the impact of their decisions and choices

---

Health Services Research Foundation Publication. Retrieved on April 27, 2008, from http://www.chsrf.ca/final_research/ogc/pdf/ doren2_final.pdf

[44] Jaworski, J. (1996). *Synchronicity: The inner path of leadership*. San Francisco, CA: Berrett-Khoeler Publishers.

[45] Department of the Army (1999). *Field manual 22-100: Army leadership -- Be, know, do*. Washington, DC: Department of the Army.

from a long-term perspective. They give less direct orders. Strategic leaders may also tend toward being transformational in their methods.

- **Organizational**: Organizational leaders bridge the gap between the direct and strategic leader. Organizational leaders influence a set of sub-teams, without direct contact with the majority of their down-line employees. At the organizational level, the European Foundation for Quality Management defines organizational leadership as "how leaders develop and facilitate the achievement of the mission and vision, develop values required for long-term success and implement these via appropriate actions and behaviors, and are personally involved in ensuring that the organization's management system is developed and implemented."[46] The organizational leader focuses on operationalizing the strategy through medium-term outcomes as well as processes and innovation. To achieve their mission, plans are developed and implemented through the allocation of resources.

- **Direct**: Direct leaders use face-to-face continuous contact with those under their command. This leader works at the tactical level. Direct leaders are typically subject matter experts in their team's domains of knowledge and skill used in functioning and achieving their mission, goals, and objectives. The orders they give are more specific and definitively time-bound. Their focus is more in the here and now and thus their perspective is more in the near–term timeframe. Their span of control is smaller; therefore, the consequences of their actions are relatively contained and with less collateral damage. The direct leader is more apt to follow a process consistently and adhere strictly to the rules.

The commonality of these three leadership levels is these leaders all influence the actions of people; however, their difference lies in each level's perspective. The difference in perspectives dictates how the specific leader achieves their mission. Regardless of the level of leadership, leading is about relationships and behaviors. The existing relationships within the act of leading are between the influencer and the influenced. Understanding both thoughts and emotions are important too, the behavioral component of leading is about changing the actions of other people.[47]

An individual's ability to transition from one leadership type to another or from one leadership level to the next is a function of one's abstract thinking ability.

---

[46] European Foundation for Quality Management (2009). *Leadership*. Retrieved on January 18, 2016, from www.efqm.org.
[47] Mullins, L. (1996). *Management and Organizational Behavior*. London, UK: Pitman Publishing.

Leaders transitioning from direct to indirect leadership types and thus from the Direct (tactical) level to the Strategic level requires a transition from concrete to more abstract thinking. Concrete thinkers, leading at the direct level, live in the here and now and takes a more literal perspective on tasks and objectives. Abstract thinkers, leading at the strategic level, focuses on the context in which the content lays. They take more of an inductive vice a concrete deductive perspective on their leadership style.

Styles

Servant Leadership (Foundational)

The *servant leadership* style is not the latest fad of various leadership styles; it is a foundational leadership style. Servant leadership is about changing the status quo and enabling others to achieve more collectively with others than by themselves. Robert K. Greenleaf established Servant Leadership in his essay *The Servant as a Leader* published in 1970.[48] According to Greenleaf:[49]

> "The servant-leader is a servant first. It begins with the natural feeling that one wants to serve. Then conscious choice brings one to aspire to lead. The best test is: do those served grow as persons: do they, while being served, become healthier, wiser, freer, more autonomous, more likely themselves to become servants? And, what is the effect on the least privileged in society; will they benefit, or, at least, not be further deprived?"

Servant leadership is purported to be applicable for any environment.[50] It can be considered as leading by taking care of the workforce. Additionally, it is thus considered as a foundation upon which all other leadership styles rest because servant leadership is about enabling an organization's workforce, its employees, to achieve results. The genesis of *servant leadership* evolved from Greenleaf's view of a leadership crisis.[51]

The servant leader desires to serve and purports honesty and integrity as their personal value along with humility, equality, and respect for others.[52] "The first

---

[48] Greenleaf Center for Servant Leadership (n.d.). *What Is Servant Leadership?* Retrieved on January 9, 2016, from https://www.greenleaf.org/what-is-servant-leadership/
[49] Greenleaf, R. K. (1977/2002). Servant-leadership: A journey into the nature of legitimate power and greatness. Mahwah, NJ: Paulist Press.
[50] Greenleaf, R. (1977). Servant leadership: A journey into the nature of legitimate power and greatness. New York, NY: Paulist Press.
[51] Greenleaf, R. (1978). The leadership crisis in L. Spears (ed.), *The power of servant leadership*. San Francisco, CA: Berrett-Koehler.
[52] Russell, R. (2001). The role of values in servant leadership. *Leadership and Organization Development*, 22 (2), 76-83.

impulse for a servant leader is to listen first and talk less."[53] He/she lives for serving those people within their sphere of influence. Their greatest pleasure centers on attending to the needs of the people within their sphere of influence; they focus on these people's well-being. A servant leader "assists people in being their best, coaches and assists in their personal growth, listens well and builds community."[54] They help these people to grow cognitively, behaviorally, and emotionally. Servant leaders have a strong ethical compass. There compass' needle points to focusing on their followers' needs.[55] Their own self-interest is the farthest thought on their minds. The end state of their followers' lives, besides being better people, is they may desire to become servant leaders themselves.

At a higher level, Robert Greenleaf expressed in another essay, *The Institution as Servant*, the ultimate objective of his concept of servant leadership is the creation of a better community and society.[56] "Servant leadership emphasizes increased service to others, a holistic approach to work, promoting a sense of community and the sharing of power in decision making."[57] The better community and society could be defined as being kinder with everyone, and working for the betterment of others.

Some well-known individuals who exude servant leadership are:

- **Abraham Lincoln:** Lincoln served to preserve the United States of America and to dismantle the institution of slavery.[58]
- **Martin Luther King, Jr.:** King thrived to improve the quality of life for Americans with cultural heritages as to be from such places as Africa, in the form of a civil rights activist.[59]
- **Nelson Mandela:** Mandela went to jail for his principles regarding equality for all South Africans.[60][61]

---

[53] Lubin, K. (2001). *Visionary leader behaviors and their congruency with servant leadership characteristics*. Dissertation Abstracts International, 62(08), 2645. (UMI No. 3022943)

[54] Servant Leadership. Retrieved on January 10, 2016, from http://www.leadersdirect.com/servant.html

[55] Pollard, C. (1996). *The soul of the firm*. Grand Rapids, MI: Harper Business and Zondervan Publishing House.

[56] Greenleaf, R. K. (1976). *The institution as servant*. Indianapolis, IN: Robert K. Greenleaf Center.

[57] Spears L. & Lawrence M. (2004). Practicing servant leadership: Succeeding through trust, bravery, and forgiveness. San Francisco: Wiley.

[58] Hubbard, C.M. (May 31, 2011). *Lincoln as a servant leader*. Retrieved on January 10, 2016, from http://lincolninstitute.wordpress.com/2011/05/31/lincoln-as-a-servant-leader/

[59] Perry, J. (January 18, 2010). *Martin Luther King, Jr: A true servant leader*. Retrieved on January 10, 2016, from http://www.huffingtonpost.com/james-perry/martin-luther-king-jr-a-t_b_427417.html

[60] Medhin, S. (n.d.). *Servant leadership: A leadership style whose time has come*. Retrieved on January 10, 2016, from http://www.aigaforum.com/articles/Servant_Leadership_Style.pdf

[61] Freed, J. (2013). Remembering Nelson Mandela: A true servant leader. Retrieved on January 10, 2016, from http://www.jannfreed.com/2013/12/remembering-nelson-mandela-a-true-servant-leader.html

- **Mahatma Gandhi:** Gandhi lived his life to liberate India from colonialism through peaceful resistance.[62]

The above list of servant leaders may be quite daunting because one may not relate to them. Many ordinary people abide by the cognitions, behaviors, and emotions defining a servant leader. These ordinary servant leaders can be identified if one knows what to look for.

What are the overarching themes through which the identifying specifics of servant leadership is based? These themes include valuing people, developing people, building a community, displaying authenticity, providing leadership, and sharing leadership. The descriptions of the overarching themes for servant leadership are:[63]

- **Valuing People**: Servant leaders believe people are important and should be appreciated. People are not a resource to be used for the benefit of the leader. A servant leader's behaviors depict displaying activities focused on meeting the needs of others so the others can achieve optimal performance. The process for learning what the needs of others are is through listening non-judgmentally and actively.

- **Developing People**: Servant leaders believe for other people to reach their full potential they should be nurtured and assisted in their personal and professional growth. They provide a safe environment in which an atmosphere promoting learning and rewarding risk taking flourishes. This growth is accomplished through the servant leader modeling the desired behaviors to others. The servant leader works alongside the others to encourage and mentor them along the way.

- **Building Community**: Servant leaders believe in the power of the team. The optimal team works from a perspective of a shared vision and mission and a focus of common goals and objectives. The strength of the team is based upon the strength of the team members' relationships. Servant leader's behaviors depict activities designed to create an environment whereas all wants to work together and learn to support each other for the betterment of the whole team. Servant leaders promotes the strength of diversity and differences.

---

[62] Ibid.
[63] Laub, J. (1999). Assessing the servant organization: Development of the servant organizational leadership assessment (SOLA) instrument. *Dissertation Abstracts International, 60* (02), 308. (UMI No. 9921922)

- **Displaying Authenticity**: Servant leaders believe leaders are genuine, open, and approachable to others. A servant leader's behaviors depict transparency and they hold themselves accountable to all in a accepting and trusting environment. If they make a mistake, they readily assume responsibility for it.

- **Providing Leadership**: Servant leaders believe in action and taking on initiatives while influencing others to do the same. They are oriented to the future; they envision what can be and should be. Servant leader's behaviors depict their desire to make an impact. They enable people and organizations to strive toward and to achieve optimal performance.

- **Sharing Leadership**: Servant leaders believe in accomplishing goals and objectives by enabling in others their leadership knowledge, skills, and abilities to emerge. They promote the development of healthy, high-performance organizations and understand from a gestalt perspective, the whole will achieve greater results than the sum of the parts. Servant leader's behaviors depict the ability to brainstorm solutions, make decisions, and develop and implement plans. They create and utilize performance metrics and utilize them to ensure results are achieved.

What are the identifying specifics of servant leadership? The major attributes from Greenleaf's writings[64] and identified accompanying attributes of servant leadership are:[65]

Major Attributes	
• Listening	• Conceptualization
• Empathy	• Foresight
• Healing	• Stewardship
• Awareness	• Commitment to the Growth of People
• Persuasion	• Building Community

---

[64] Spears, L. (1998). Tracing the growing impact of servant leadership, in L.C. Spears (ed.), *Insights on leadership: Service, stewardship, spirit, and servant-leadership.* New York, NY: John Wiley and Sons.

[65] Russell, R., & Stone, G. (2002). A review of servant leadership attributes: Developing a practical model. *Leadership & Organization Development Journal,* 23(3), 145-157.

The definitions explaining each of the major servant leadership attributes are:[66]

- **Listening** (p.2): Servant leaders are listeners. Effective listening is being in tune to both verbal and non-verbal signals as well as having the ability to understand the message. In addition, the servant leader must be aware of and understand their own thoughts and feelings. Organizationally, servant leaders listen to the team and determine what is being communicated.

- **Empathy** (p.3): Servant leaders are compassionate and accept people for who they are. They are able to understand other's thoughts, behaviors, and emotions because they are able to put themselves in the other's world. They accept their organization and the individuals in which it is comprised with both strengths and weaknesses.

- **Healing** (p.3): Servant leaders works to enable others to live a fulfilled life. They enable others to grow as well as overcome situations, issues, and problems limiting their ability to maximize their performance. They strengthen or heal relationships within an organization to improve its performance.

- **Awareness** (p.3): Servant leaders view situations, issues, and problems from a comprehensive and universal perspective. They see a follower's environment holistically as integrated components. They are able to view and understand the situations, issues, and problems facing an organization.

- **Persuasion** (p.3): Servant leaders lead not from a position of authority but rather from encouraging, coaxing, influencing, and convincing others on what the followers should do. From an organizational perspective, they use their skills to achieve consensus.

- **Conceptualization** (p.3): Servant leaders see situations, issues, and problems abstractly. Their vision's foundation is based upon a futuristic view of the possibilities. They think beyond the current day and sees what can be tomorrow. Organizationally, they are strategic but are able to balance it with the tactical.

- **Foresight** (p.3): Servant leaders leverage understanding of the past and combine it with knowledge of the present then apply this information to make decisions for the future. They make informed decisions with the propensity of making correct decisions. In essence, they make data based decisions as organizational leaders.

---

[66] Spears, L. (n.d.). On Character and Servant-Leadership: Ten Characteristics of Effective, Caring Leaders. Retrieved on January 10, 2016, from http://www.greenleaf.org/

- **Stewardship** (p.4): Servant leaders are agents of their followers by living to meet their followers' needs. They stress the use of persuasion and consensus rather than control and a position of authority. As an organizational leader, they hold themselves accountable for the positions of trust they embrace.
- **Commitment to the growth of people** (p.4): Servant leaders are extremely dedicated to the development of their followers. They encourage their followers to be active participants in their future. They actively nurture the personal and professional growth of these individuals for the betterment of the organization.
- **Building community** (p.4): Servant leaders actively pursue the development of teamwork to create a sense of belonging. This action ensures the organization works as one to achieve goals and objectives because the followers have garnered buy-in and ownership in them.

Environmental Leadership (Strategic Leadership Level)

The *strategic leadership level* refers to an organization's leaders who express a strategic vision for the holistic organization based on the state of the environmental forces then inspire and influence others to acquire and claim the vision as their own. Additionally, based upon the strategic vision, the strategic leader's scope includes creating organizational structure and allocating resources necessary to accomplish the strategic vision. They work in an ambiguous environment on very difficult issues influencing and influenced by the organizations internal and external forces. *Strategic leadership* requires the potential to foresee and comprehend the work environment. It requires objectivity and potential to look at the broader picture. Strategic leaders create vision, express vision, passionately possess vision, and persistently drives to achieve the vision.

A few main traits of effective *strategic leadership* leading to organizational high performance includes:

- **Being loyal**: Powerful and effective leaders demonstrate their loyalty to their vision by their words and actions.
- **Keeping informed**: Efficient and effective leaders keep themselves updated about what is happening within their organization. They have various formal and informal sources of information in the organization.
- **Using power judiciously**: Strategic leaders makes a very wise use of their power. They play the power game skilfully and develop consent for their ideas rather than forcing their ideas upon others. They push their ideas gradually.

- **Having a wider perspective or outlook**: Strategic leaders have skills in their narrow specialty but they also have knowledge about other areas.
- **Being motivated**: Strategic leaders have a zeal for work going beyond money and power; they also have energy and determination toward enabling others to achieve goals.
- **Having compassion**: Strategic leaders understand the views and feelings of their subordinates, and make decisions after considering them.
- **Having self-control**: Strategic leaders have the potential to control distracting/disturbing moods and desires; they think before acting.
- **Having Social skills**: Strategic leaders must be friendly and social.
- **Having self-awareness**: Strategic leaders have the potential to understand their own moods and emotions as well as their impact on others.
- **Being ready to delegate and authorize**: Effective leaders are proficient at delegation. They are aware delegation avoids the overloading of responsibilities on the leaders. They also recognize authorizing subordinates to make decisions will motivate them immensely.
- **Articulating**: Strong leaders are articulate enough to communicate the vision of where the organization is heading to the organizational members in terms obtaining buy-in and ownership by those members.
- **Being constant and reliable**: Strategic leaders constantly convey their vision until it becomes a component of organizational culture.

Viewing the holistic organization through the lens of the *environment leadership style*, the organization is a complex adaptive system and is not controlled to the same utility as a machine. Some of the attributes of a machine are they contain metal and bolts, wires and circuit boards as well as switches and knobs. Machines have inputs and outputs with some type of processing in-between. Machines are static devices. On the other hand, people comprise organizations; therefore, organizations are dynamic with many forces operating internally and externally to it. The challenge is the forces are unseen; however, the results of these forces are visible. These forces are presented as the environment in which the organization works. As the organization's environment changes, so must the cognitions, behaviors, and emotions of the organization if it is to remain a viable and competitive entity within its industry sector.

Linear strategies, for the most part, are irrelevant and ineffective because of the dynamic nature of the environmental forces playing on the organization. One should remember people comprise organizations. When people are involved, human nature and the consequence of the natural order of competitiveness as well as the psychological theory of Abraham Maslow with his hierarchy of needs are also a component of the environmental forces. This environmental variability of forces introduces a hint or the view of unpredictability or seemingly the perception of randomness occurring in and on the organization. However, because of the environmental variability and the interaction between all of the forces at play internal and external to the organization, the *strategic leadership* level of an organization should present more adaptive, innovative, evolving, and non-linear solutions. Understanding the holistic nature of the environmental variability of forces coupled with non-linear solutions is essential in providing leadership at the strategic level so to have a greater propensity in achieving a desired future state. For these reasons, an *environmental leadership style* is appropriate at the *strategic leadership level*.

The *environmental leadership style* is transformational by nature. This transformational nature focuses on making change happen in primarily in the organization. Optimally, it is about creating positive change so to increase the organization's value proposition with its stakeholders, such as customers, employees, and vendors. Additionally, it is about developing organizational leaders from within the organization by enhancing motivation, morale, and performance. This transformational nature includes molding employees to connect their own identity with that of the organization's identity. This concept is not unlike how a civilian coming into the military service is transformed during Basic Training from being and thinking like a civilian to adopting the military thoughts, behaviors, emotions, and values.

"Most transformation programs satisfy themselves with shifting the same old furniture about in the same old room. Some seek to throw some of the furniture away. But, real transformation requires that we design the room itself. Perhaps even, blow up the old room. It requires that we change the thinking behind our thinking – literally that we learn to rewire our corporate brains."[67]

The transformational nature of the *environmental leadership style* changes or molds those in the organization to meet the forces acting on the organization with the end state being the continuance of the organization to be viable and competitive based on the environment in which it operates. Environmental leaders enable everyone in the organization to advance to a higher level.[68] As Lester Thurow, an American political economist and a former dean of the MIT Sloan School of

---

[67] Zohar, D. (1990). *The quantum self: Human nature and consciousness defined by the new physics.* New York, NY: William Morrow

[68] Burns, J. (1978). *Leadership*, New York, NY: Harper and Row.

Management stated, "A competitive world offers two possibilities. You can lose. Or, if you want to win, you can change."

Being transformational as an element of the *environmental leadership style* is important because without it, people will not adapt and organizations will diminish. Transformational means creating an organizational culture striving to move beyond and not accepting the status quo. This culture does not accept the way things always have been done as the best and only way of doing it. The culture strives to constantly create and innovate; the culture believes there may be better way. In 1961, Bobby Kennedy, the Former Attorney General stated, "Some men see things the way they are and ask why. I see things as they could be and ask why not?"

The transformational nature of environmental leaders has four elements:[69]

1. **Individualized Consideration** – The degree the leader takes care of organizational needs and listens to the workforce's concerns. The leader gives empathy and support, keeps communication open and places challenges before the organization. This endeavor also encompasses the need for respect and celebrates the individual contribution the members make to the holistic organization.

2. **Intellectual Stimulation** – The degree the leader challenges assumptions, takes risks, and solicits the organization for ideas. The leader stimulates and encourages creativity within the organizational rank-and-file. They nurture and develop the individuals who think independently. Learning is a value and unexpected situations are viewed as opportunities to learn. The employees ask questions, think deeply about their duties and responsibilities and figure out better ways to execute their tasks.

3. **Inspirational Motivation** – The degree to which the leader articulates an appealing and inspirational vision. Leaders with inspirational motivation challenge the organization with high standards, communicate optimism about future goals, and provide meaning for all within the organization. The organizational workforce with a strong sense of purpose is motivated to act. Purpose and meaning provide the energy that drives the organization forward. The visionary aspects of leadership are supported by communication skills making the vision understandable, precise, powerful, and engaging. The workforce is willing to invest more effort in their tasks, they are encouraged and optimistic about the future, and believe in their abilities.

---

[69] Bass, B. & Bass, R. (2008). *The Bass handbook of leadership: Theory, research, and managerial applications* (4th ed). New York: NY: Free Press.

4. **Idealized Influence** – The degree, to which the leader is a role model for instantiating high ethical behavior, instilling pride, and gaining respect and trust.

In addition to the overarching four elements above, for the environmental leader to be transformational by nature, the following tips are presented:[70]

- Develop a challenging and attractive vision, together with the employees.
- Tie the vision to a strategy for its achievement.
- Develop the vision, specify and translate it to actions.
- Express confidence, decisiveness and optimism about the vision and its implementation.
- Realize the vision through small planned steps and small successes in the path for its full implementation.

Participative Leadership (Organizational Leadership Level)

The *organizational leadership level* is the action of influencing organizational members to execute organizational change. The main objective of organizational leadership is strategic productivity. Another aim of organizational leadership is to develop an environment in which employees forecast the organization's needs in context of their own job. Organizational leaders encourage employees to innovate and follow their own ideas. Organizational leaders make use of reward and incentive systems for encouraging productive and quality employees to show much better performance for their organization.

For clarity, the *participative leadership style* is broader and deeper than the Hersey/Blanchard *situational leadership* style at the *Direct Leadership Level* presented in the next section. Within the *situational leadership* style, the relationship/maturity (R; M) forces and competency/commitment or development (D) forces are two of many influencers or forces acting in the organizational environment, which collectively are catalysts dictating the specific leadership behavior/style (S). The earlier presented business model depicts many, if not all, of these forces in a generalized perspective, of the influencers or the internal and external forces playing on the leadership situation and in the organizational environment. However, the *participative leadership style* uses an understanding of the forces at play just within the organization, then, ultimately, designing databased and action-plans to deliver solutions and results. The *participative leadership style* indicates the level of behavior required of the leader to direct, motivate, guide, and lead teams so to more effectively and efficiently achieve the desired outcomes.

---

[70] Yukl, G. (1999). An evaluation of conceptual weaknesses in transformational and charismatic leadership theories. *Leadership Quarterly*, 10(2), 285-305.

The concept of leadership is not static since both the internal dynamics of organizations and the external environment constantly influence it. The *organizational leader* utilizes the presented business model at a greater level of granularity in the development and implementation of their specific actions with the strategic input from the strategic leader. The *participative leadership style* is concerned with blending and filling the gap between the tactical, *direct leader* and the more abstract, *strategic leader*. It, subsequently, is appropriate for the *organizational leader level*.

The objective of using the *participative leadership style* at the *organizational leader level* is to create lasting change within an organization. To initiate change and drive the internal organization toward high performance, the *organizational leader* must understand the organizational internal workings. Additionally, they must understand the holistic complex adaptive system, called the organization, and thus, the interrelationship between and among each component, as depicted by the Business Model.

For every organization, a developed and implemented plan is designed perfectly to get the results it is getting. The leader's activity is to evaluate if the results obtained are those desired. If so, then perfect. However, if the obtained results are not desired or not quite hitting the mark, then a reevaluation is in order to determine what changes are necessary in the organization or the plan so to obtain the desired results. From this perspective, the *participative leadership style* takes on a more path-goal nature while driving toward high performance.

The path-goal nature focuses on the organizational leader adjusting cognitions, behaviors, and emotions to best suit the culture of the organization to most effectively and efficiently obtain the desired results.[71][72][73] The ultimate goal is to motivate, empower, and, otherwise, create a high-level of employee engagement to insure the results align with the direction toward which the strategic leader is transforming the organization. The path-goal nature is particularly effective in overcoming resistance to change because it enables the organizational leader the flexibility to adjust as necessary to achieve results.

The path-goal nature of organizational leadership utilizing a participative leadership style utilizes a generalized process of steps. These steps are:

1. **Evaluate the Organization** – Determine the culture and other characteristics of the workforce. This evaluation explores the

---

[71] Evans, M. (1970). The effects of supervisory behavior on the path-goal relationship. *Organizational Behavior and Human Performance*. 5(3), 277–298.

[72] House, R., & Mitchell, T. (1974). Path-goal theory of leadership. *Journal of Contemporary Business*. 3(4), 81–97.

[73] Northouse, P. (2013). Leadership Theory and Practice. Thousand Oaks, CA: Sage Publications.

experience and ability level of the workforce as well as the leaders own perception and that of the workforce's locus of control.

2. **Determine the Participative Leadership Level** – Dependent upon the evaluation, the organizational leader will select an appropriate participative level. Figure 4 depicts the variance between the participative leadership levels. The levels go from low to high and correlate with the Hersey/Blanchard Situational Leadership model of behavior/style of S1 to S4 respectively, which is presented in the *situational leadership* style at the *direct leadership level*.

3. **Enable the Employees** – The organizational leader through the fast array of leadership knowledge, skills, abilities, other characteristics he/she has within their leadership kitbag, they, through the holistic organizational team, will strive to achieve the desired results.

As seen in Figure 4, the *participative leadership style* deals with control and one's perception of how much control they give to others. At one anchor point, the autocratic participative level requires high control, while on the other anchor point, the laissez faire *participative leadership style* implies low control. There are also multiple levels in-between the anchor points.[74]

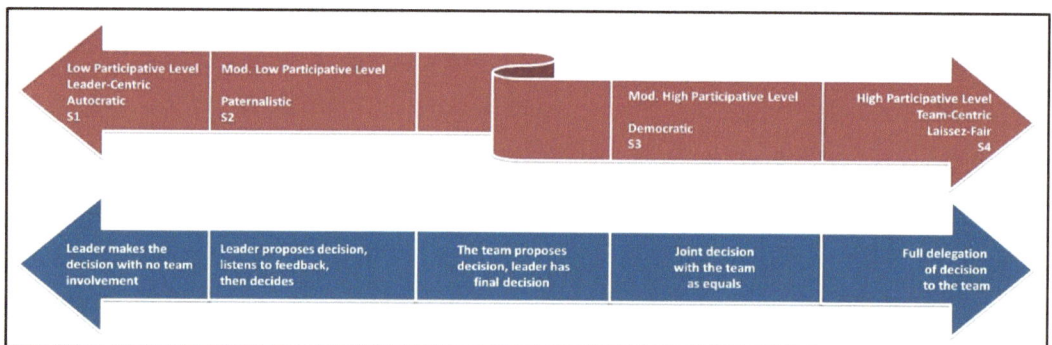

Figure 4: The Participative Leadership Levels Defined

The low participative level, equating also to an autocratic leader, clear direction and expectations are provided to the organization to achieve the desired results. This participative level focuses on two elements, the leader's command over the organization and their control over the workforce. This participative level requires the leader to assume control of the decision-making. This participative level is best used when there is a short of time or where the leader is truly the subject matter expert.

The moderately high participative level, equating to a more democratic leader, is one whereas the holistic team determines the best course of action through which to achieve the desired results. Many times this participative level generates the best

---

[74]Lewin, K., Lippit, R., & White, R. (1939). Patterns of aggressive behavior in experimentally created social climates. Journal of Social Psychology, 10(2), 271-301.

action plans though they are realized in a greater length of time. It enables the workforce to participate as equals in the decision-making process and allows for more discussion; the end state is a higher quality decision being made, which has a greater degree of commitment, ownership, and buy-in for the decision by the workforce.

The high participative level, correlating to a laissez-fair methodology, enables the workforce to determine the best course of action. The success of this high participative level is a function of the relationships between, and maturity levels of the workforce as well as their competency, commitment or development levels. There is little to no leadership guidance at this participative level, which leaves decision-making up to the holistic organization team. This level is best utilized when the organizational team situation involves highly qualified and motivated members all striving to work together to create the best solution driving toward high performance. If this situation does not exist, the results tend toward the organizational team members blaming the others for mistakes and failures, refusing to accept their own responsibility in creating the mistakes and failures, and producing the slowest progress and work toward achieving the desired results.

Situational Leadership (Direct Leadership Level)

The *Direct leadership level* is about using inventiveness, perception, and planning to assist an individual in realizing the organizational objectives and goals. The creative direct leader, who exemplifies high performance, enables the workforce to realize its potential by the development of an environment where each person feels free and willing to contribute to organizational success. Aspects like raising job complexity, employee empowerment and time demands, together with low organizational controls such as on decision making, information flow and reward systems, will raise employee creativity.[75]

In order to empower employees to be willing and able to contribute to organizational effectiveness, leadership and teamwork procedures favoring creativity are necessary to achieve success.[76] A creative holistic workforce is committed to their work and organization, and may bring in important issues, provided top management value their work and ideas. According to a Gallup Management Journal survey, engaged employees are more likely to think outside of the box and produce creative ideas more than disengaged employees.[77] Engaged

---

[75] Adams, R. (2006). Innovation measurement: A review. *International Journal of Management Reviews*, 8 (1), 21-47.

[76] Unsworth, K. L. (2005). Creative requirement: A neglected construct in the study of employee creativity? *Group Organization Management*, 30(5), 541-560.

[77] Hartel, J., Schmidt, F., & Keyes, L. (2003). *Well-being in the workplace and its relationship with business outcomes: A review of the Gallup studies* (205-224). Washington D.C.: American Psychological Association.

employees are also more receptive to new ideas. The research concludes engaged employees tend to find and suggest new ways to improve their work and business processes, which may lead to the assumption creative employees have a deeper understanding of the organizational processes, by being in a privileged position to identify, define, and discover organizational problems.

The concept of a *situational leadership style* emerged from a series of research studies from Ohio State University and the University of Michigan in the 1950s. These studies focused upon leadership and the construct of whether leaders should be concerned more with results (tasks) or people (relationship) oriented. These universities concluded a leader's leadership style was, ultimately, a function of the situation; therefore, the leadership style is about the influencers or forces acting within the situation and environment in which the leader and the led find themselves. The Hersey/Blanchard Leadership model is about the people, accomplishing tasks, and the level of leadership participation. The *situational leadership style* is appropriate for use at the *direct leadership level*.

Most of what many seem to know about the model of *situational leadership* is possibly because of two people, namely Dr. Paul Hersey and Mr. Kenneth Blanchard. Dr. Hersey, a professor and author of *The Situational Leader*,[78] and Mr. Blanchard, a leadership trainer and author of *The One Minute Manager*,[79] worked together to develop their concept of *situational leadership* on the first edition of *Management of Organizational Behavior*.[80] A successful leader, being one achieving results with their employees using the *situational leadership* style, changes their leadership behavior based on the maturity of the people they are leading and the details of the task. Leaders place more or less emphasis on the task and more or less emphasis on the relationships with the people they are leading as a function on what is needed to get the task achieved successfully.

The *situational leadership style* purports various combinations of four relationship/maturity levels of the led (R1; M1 – R4; M4) and four competency/commitment or development levels (D1 – D4), which collective are influencers or forces dictating the specific leadership behavior/style (S1 – S4) the leader should use.[81] One of the two Hersey/Blanchard influencers or forces, based upon their situational leadership concept, is the R1; M1 – R4; M4 relationship/maturity levels. This influencer or force equates to various

---

[78] Hersey, P. (1985). *The situational leader.* New York, NY: Warner Books.
[79] Blanchard, K., & Johnson, S. (1982). *The one-minute manager.* New York, NY: William Morrow & Co.
[80] Hersey, P. & Blanchard, K. (1969). *Management of organizational behavior – Utilizing human resources.* Upper Saddle River, NJ: Prentice Hall.
[81] Blanchard, K., Zigarmi, R., & and Zigarmi, D. (1985). *Leadership and the One Minute Manager: Increasing effectiveness through situational leadership.* New York, NY: William Morrow & Co.

employee/individual team member's levels of skill, confidence, and motivation. For example, a person might be confident and motivated to do a specific task; however, if they did not possess the skills to do the tasks, they may have a relationship/maturity level of R1; M1.

- **R-1; M1**: The person lacks the specific skills and is not confident or motivated, meaning unable and unwilling, to do the tasks or to take responsibility for it.
- **R-2; M2**: The person is confident and motivated, able and willing to do the task. However, they lack the skill to accomplish the task. They are, in essence, novices.
- **R-3; M3**: The person is motivated and skilled at doing the task; however, they lack the confidence that they are capable of completing it. They are unwilling to do the task.
- **R-4; M4**: The person is skilled, confident, and motivated to accomplish the task.

The other Hersey/Blanchard influencers or forces are the various possible combinations of competency/commitment or development levels of the employees or people being led, which is measured as the D1 – D4 levels. According to Hersey, a leader's role is to develop competency/commitment levels in their workforce, in other words, the people of are led.[82] Taking Hersey's thoughts on competence and commitment, Blanchard, in his Situational Leadership II Model, defined one's competence as their level of ability, knowledge, and skill to perform a task while one's commitment was the level of confidence and motivation to perform a task. The combinations of these two constructs defines the various levels of development as a person evolves from developing to having been developed.[83] The leader's leadership style is then influenced by where the employee is at in their development level. So, the various combinations of competence and commitment equates to:

- **D1**: Low competence and high commitment
- **D2**: Low competence and low commitment
- **D3**: High competence and low/variable commitment
- **D4**: High competence and high commitment

The *situational leadership style* dictates there are leadership behavioral options (See Figure 5). With the *S* standing for *style*, the leadership behavioral style of S1 – S4 is influenced by the M1 - M4, and D1 – D4 levels. The leadership style of S1 – S4 respectively equate to:

---

[82] Hersey, P. (1985). *The situational leader.* New York, NY: Warner Books.
[83] Blanchard, K., Zigarmi, R., & and Zigarmi, D. (1985). *Leadership and the One Minute Manager: Increasing effectiveness through situational leadership.* New York, NY: William Morrow & Co.

- **S1: Telling** – Focuses on one-way communications, whereas the leader tells the people specifically all of the activity's components. This behavior aligns more with the Autocratic leadership method.
- **S2: Selling** – Focuses on one-way communications, whereas the leader sells the people on the activity's components in an attempt to convince them to perform the task. This behavior aligns more with the Paternalistic leadership method.
- **S3: Participating** – Focuses on performing the activity's components with the people in an attempt to show them how to do the task and being one of the team. This behavior aligns more with the Democratic leadership method.
- **S4: Delegating** – Focuses on trusting the people and team to accomplish the activity's components while monitoring their progress. This behavior aligns more with the Laissez-fair leadership method.

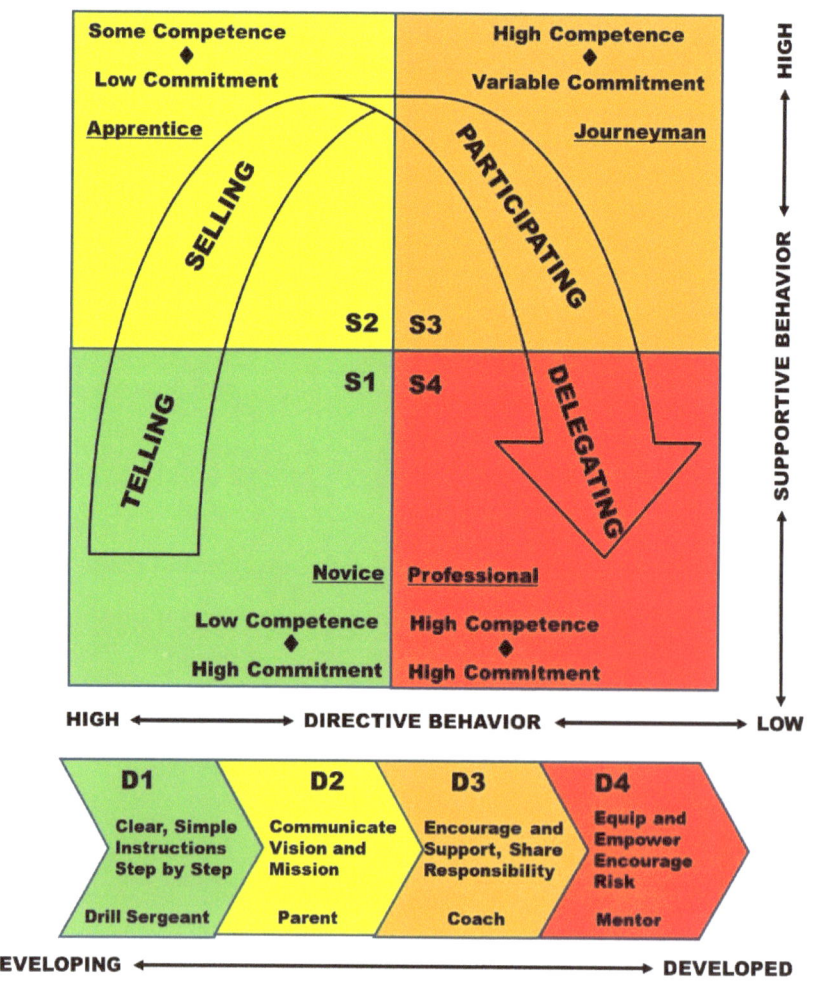

Figure 5: Situational Leadership Curve

Conclusion

The *Servant Leadership Style* is foundational and is people-centered. "Doing menial chores does not necessarily indicate a servant leader. Instead a servant leader is one who invests in enabling others, in helping them be and do their best."[84] They promote a positive leader-follower relationship within their organizations.[85] Promoting servant leadership will enable a greater number of leaders to realize its benefits in their organization. Employee learning implements the empowerment process; the organizational leaders must teach and mirror the cognitions, behaviors, and emotions to the employees so the employees will do the same to the customers.[86] Robert Greenleaf proposed a servant leadership model for employee empowerment leading to employee and customer satisfaction.[87] Servant leaders focus on the needs of others more so than the organization's vision, mission, goals, and objectives. By focusing on the employees of the organization, the concept is, they ensure the organization is successful.[88] The ten attributes of servant leadership lay the cognitive, behavioral, and emotional foundation within organizations with the end state being high performance. The *Servant Leadership Style* is the foundation upon which the other leadership styles rest.

Those individuals, at the *Strategic Leadership Level* using the *environmental leadership style,* are transformational by nature. This transformational nature focuses on making change happen in primarily in the organization. The strategic leaders are those focused on developing a strategic vision for the holistic organization based on the state of the environmental forces. They are charged with inspiring and influencing others to accept as well as assume ownership and buy-in for the vision. Additionally, the strategic leader is responsible for laying the organizational foundation upon the strategic vision and will, while allocating the necessary resources to accomplish the strategic vision. Optimally, strategic leaders create positive change so to increase the organization's value proposition with its stakeholders, such as customers, employees, and vendors. They work in the land of ambiguity and a myriad of forces influencing and influenced by the organization. Strategic leaders create vision, express vision, passionately possess vision, and persistently drives to achieve the vision.

---

[84] Hall, A. (1991). Why a great leader. In K. Hall, *Living Leadership: Biblical Leadership Speaks to Our Day*. Anderson, IN: Warner Press.

[85] Bass, B. (1990). Bass & Stogdill's handbook of leadership: Theory, research, & managerial applications (3rd ed.). New York, NY: The Free Press.

[86] Spencer, B. (1994). Models of organization and total quality management: A comparison and critical evaluation. *Academy of Management Review*, 19(3), 446-471.

[87] Greenleaf, R. K. (1977/2002). Servant-leadership: A journey into the nature of legitimate power and greatness. Mahwah, NJ: Paulist Press.

[88] Stone, A., Russell R., & Patterson, K. (2004). Transformational versus servant leadership: A difference in leader focus. *Leadership & Organization Development Journal*, 24(3/4), 349-361.

The leaders, at the *Organizational Leadership Level* using the *Participative Leadership Style,* are primarily concerned with blending and filling the gap between the tactical, *direct leader* and the more abstract, *strategic leader.* The main objective of using the *participative leadership style* at the *organizational leader level* is to create lasting change within an organization. The *participative leadership style* leverages an understanding of the forces action on and within the organization to develop and implement action-plans delivering the desired future state. The *participative leadership style* indicates the level of behavior required of the leader to direct, motivate, guide, and lead teams so to more effectively and efficiently achieve the desired outcomes. Every organization is designed perfectly to deliver the current results. It is incumbent upon the organizational leader to evaluate the results and determine if there are desired or not. The outcome determination dictates if adjustments in the plan is necessary.

Lastly, but by no means least, the leaders, at the *Direct Leadership Level* instituting a *Situational Leadership Style,* are in essence where the rubber meets the road. The leaders at the direct level use inventiveness, perception, and planning to enable the realization of the organizational objectives and goals. The creative direct leader, exemplifying high performance, empowers the workforce to excel and realize their potential by the development of an environment where people feel free and willing to contribute to organizational success. Most of what many seem to know about the model of *situational leadership* is possibly because of two people, namely Dr. Paul Hersey and Mr. Kenneth Blanchard. A successful leader, being one achieving results with their employees using the *situational leadership* style, changes their leadership behavior based on the maturity of the people they are leading and the details of the task. Leaders place more or less emphasis on the task and more or less emphasis on the relationships with the people they are leading as a function on what is needed to get the task achieved successfully.

In conclusion, high performance leaders, utilizing effective leadership techniques, are essential for organizations to achieve their strategic vision and mission as well as its business goals, and objectives.[89] The more challenging the industry is in which the organization must operate then the more critical it is to have effective leadership for the organization's success.[90] No matter what industry, for an organization to be successful in it, their customers' needs must be met or exceeded; hence, their customer satisfaction must remain high. For highly satisfied customers to exist, the organization's employees must be willing and motivated to

---

[89] Politis, J. (2003). QFD: The role of various leadership styles. *Leadership & Organization Development Journal*, 24(4), 181-193.

[90] Chien, M. (2004). A Study to Improve Organizational Performance: A View from SHRM. *Journal of American Academy of Business*, 4(1/2), 289-291.

take care of their customers. To take care of customers, the organization's employees must be empowered to do so. The appropriate use of the traits and activities at the *Foundational, Strategic, Organizational,* and *Direct Leadership Level* as presented with the *Servant, Environmental, Participative,* and *Situational Leadership Styles* respectively will empower employees to create highly satisfied customers and thus will achieve their organization's strategic vision and mission as well as its business goals and objectives.

Chapter 5:
The Organizational Science

Introduction

A leader strives to achieve the organization's vision and mission through goals and objectives. The ability of individuals to set goals, stay focused upon the related tasks leading to achieving their goals, and how well the individual performs these related tasks is irrevocably associated with how well the organization is performing.[91]

Outcomes have been historically the focus when exploring an organization's performance. Goals and mission achievements are normally associated with how well a team performs. How well the organizational members independently work and engage each other as they strive toward the overall and desired end state through such psychological constructs related to cognitions, behavior, and affections is the measuring tape for team performance and success (Marks, Mathieu, & Zaccaro, 2001).[92] [93]

A Gestalt concept states an organization's top achievements can exceed the mere sum of the parts. The overall goals met are greater than the sum of each individual team member's contribution when the organization is orchestrated by a common vision with strong internal relationships.[94] An organization's performance depicts the power of the organization's unified performance over the possibilities of the individuals comprising the organization.[95] [96]

Performance is linked to individual skills and inter-team communications.[97] Supervisors, employees, and team members have to adapt their behavior, and one clearly could say their cognitions, to change with the times and be successful.[98] This

---

[91] Phillips, J. (2000). The role of decision influence and team performance in member self-efficacy, withdrawal, satisfaction with the leader, and willingness to return. *Organizational Behavior and Human Decision Processes*, 84(1), 122-147.

[92] Devine, D., & Philips, J. (2001). Do smarter teams do better? A meta-analysis of cognitive ability and team performance. *Small Group Research*, 32(5), 507-532.

[93] Marks, M., Mathieu, J., & Zaccaro, S. (2001). A temporally based framework and taxonomy of team processes. *Academy of Management Review*, 26(3), 356-376.

[94] Ibid.

[95] Gibson, C. (1999). Do they do what they believe they can? Group efficacy and group effectiveness across tasks and cultures. *Academy of Management Journal*, 42(2), 138-152.

[96] Prussia, G., & Kinicki, A. (1996). A motivational investigation of group effectiveness using social-cognitive theory. *Journal of Applied Psychology*, 81(2), 187-198.

[97] Pincus, J. (1986). Communication satisfaction, job satisfaction, and job performance. *Human Communication Research*, 12(3), 395-419.

[98] Silverthorne, C., & Wang, T. (2001). Situational leadership style as a predictor of success and productivity among Taiwanese business organizations. *The Journal of Psychology: Interdisciplinary and Applied*, 135(4), 399-412.

constant state of change and flux can be extremely stressful.[99] [100] However, regardless of how stressful change can be, clearly individuals must change. Individuals must adapt to their current work environment to remain competitive with their peers. From a systemic perspective, if the individuals are changing so are the organizations.[101] Organizations must adapt to survive. Those surviving companies, able to still achieve goals because of their high organizational performance, could easily be considered at the top of their industry.

The state of striving for and developing peak performance is a learning organization.[102] A high performing organization is one not having any underlying issues inhibiting their ability to achieve their strategic goals in the most efficient manner possible. This definition does not imply low performing organizations do not accomplish their goals. They may! However, are organizations accomplishing their goals in the most efficient manner possible? Imagine a bicycle with rusty pedals and wheels with a rusty chain. The rider will still get to where he or she are going in spite of the rust but a rider on well-oiled and rust free pedals, wheels, and chain will get to the same point faster and with less effort. The latter is analogous of a high performing organization.

There are other factors, other than well-oiled pedals, wheels, and chain making a high performing organization.[103] One needs to explore the high and low performing organizations from a holistic perspective. This holistic perspective equates to taking a multi-view perspective, a 360-degree perspective, to most assess effectively an organization thoroughly. There are physical, cognitive, behavioral, and social attributes, to name just a few.

To tie all of these points together, all organizations should want to strive for high performance leading to optimum success. Many factors are correlated to an organization's ability to reach this point in their lifespan. To assist an organization in this endeavor, they need to know where they are in order to get to where they want to be.

There are a tremendous amount of pressures, forces, and other factors from a psychology and physics perspective influencing how well an organization is performing. Some of pressures, forces, and other factors focus around time, energy,

---

[99] Brotheridge, C. (2003). The role of fairness in mediating the effects of voice and justification on stress and other outcomes in a climate of organizational change. *International Journal of Stress Management*, 10(3), 253-268.

[100] Vakola, M., & Nikolaou, I. (2005). Attitudes towards organizational change: What is the role of employees' stress and commitment?. *Employee Relations*, 27(2), 160 - 174.

[101] Senge, P. (2006). *The fifth discipline: The art and practice of the learning organization* (2nd ed). New York, NY: Random House.

[102] Ibid.

[103] Kelloway, E. K., & Day, A. (2005). Building healthy workplaces: Where we need to be. *Canadian Journal of Behavioural Science*, 37(4), 309-298.

force, mass, momentum, and motivation. An organizational leader should understand the dynamics of these pressures or factors as they relate to optimally driving toward success by building and leveraging high performance organizations. Providing an understanding these pressures or factors influencing an organization as its leader is driving toward success is the purpose of this section. Therefore, the following universal psychology and physics theories and laws are presented by taking the known and applying them will provide understanding on *The Organizational Science* leading to high performance.

The Organization

Organizations are a collaborative effort of at least two individuals interacting together to achieve a mutual goal.[104] An individual, working alone, could not achieve these goals easily or effectively, as they require the abilities of more than one individual. To achieve goals with teams, there are multiple dynamics at play. There are the social psychology theories of relationship building and the bonds generated. There are cognitive, behavioral, affective psychology aspects as related to such areas as decision making, motivation, conflict management, goal setting, and project management to name a few. There are systemic issues. The simple fact is individuals are not only interacting within their specific environments but the team members have a work environment too. Then, the organization, as a whole, interacts with other elements so there are external systemic issues too.[105][106] All systems have common cognitive, behavioral, and affective properties. The system of interest in this book is the complex adaptive system, called the organization. The hypothesis is organizational issues, situations, or problems can be overcome with the implementation of these universal laws of organizational performance. Put another way, the premise is there exists basic laws of organizational nature associated with psychology and physics through which to determine the performance of any organization.

---

[104] Baker, D., & Salas, E. (1997). Principles and measuring teamwork: A summary and look toward the future. In M. T. Brannick, E. Salas, & C. Prince (Eds.), *Team performance assessment and measurement: Theory, methods, and applications* (pp. 331-355). Mahwah, NJ: Erlbaum.

[105] Kozlowski, S., & Bell, B. (2003). Work groups and teams in organizations. In W. C. Borman & D. R. Ilgen (Eds.), *Handbook of psychology: Industrial and organizational psychology* (Vol. 12, pp. 333-375). New York, NY: Wiley.

[106] Kozlowski, S., & Klein, K. (2000). A multilevel approach to theory and research in organizations: Contextual, temporal, and emergent processes. In K. J. Klein & S. W. J. Kozlowski (Eds.), *Multilevel theory, research, and methods in organizations* (pp. 3-90). San Francisco, CA: Jossey-Bass.

The Psychology

"The most precious commodity with which the Army deals is the individual soldier
who is the heart and soul of our combat forces."

General J. Lawton Collins

VII Corps Commander, World War II

(Department of the Army, 1999; p. 1-1)

If the above quote from a military man is translated into civilian talk, it would easily transform into expressing the heart and soul of any organization is the human capital with which makes it possible to operate. Organizational leaders quite often do not seem to consider this point. They seem so focused on the Profit-Loss Margin; they forget about the people making it possible to operate optimally at a high performance level.

Merriam-Webster defines *psychology* as the study of mind and behavior in relation to a particular field of knowledge or activity.[107] To build upon this definition, *psychology* is the scientific study of the human mind and its functions, especially those affecting behavior in a given context. The American Psychological Association indicates one psychology career is in Industrial/Organizational (I/O) Psychology. I/O psychologists apply psychological principles and research methods to the organizational workplace in the interest of improving performance, productivity, health, and the quality of work life.

An industrial/organizational (I/O) psychologist applies psychological principles and research methods to the work place. An I/O psychologist, in general, is interested in improving and understanding individual behavior and experience in organizational settings.[108] Industrial / organizational (I/O) psychologists view the world and studies research problems from a people point of view.[109] They study organizational structure and organizational change; workers' productivity and job satisfaction; consumer behavior; selection, placement, training, and development of personnel; and the interaction between humans and machines. Their responsibilities, on the job, include research, analysis, and problem solving. Many serve as human resource specialists, helping organizations with staffing, training, and employee development. Others work as management consultants in such areas as strategic planning, quality management, and coping with organizational change.

---

[107] Merriam-Webster (n.d.). *Psychology – Definition*. Retrieved on February 19, 2017, from https://www.merriam-webster.com/dictionary/psychology

[108] Society of Industrial and Organizational Psychology (SIOP; 2009). *Definition of an I/O Psychologist*. Retrieved on January 30, 2011, from http://www.siop.org/tip/tip.aspx

[109] Ibid

Alternatively, they might advise leaders on how to develop programs to identify the staff with management potential or administer a counseling service for employees on career development and preparation for retirement. Specifically, the field of I/O Psychology breaks down into seven primary areas: personnel selection, training, performance appraisal, leadership, work motivation, work attitudes, and organizational issues.[110][111][112][113]

I/O psychologists explicitly acknowledge the importance of considering the whole work system. For example, they conduct research at the organizational and team levels as well as at the individual level.[114] In addition, they formally address the corporate factors influencing work, such as labor markets, economic conditions, and governmental regulations. In fact, operating within a systems approach to understanding people at work has allowed I/O psychologists to contribute to cutting-edge issues in the design of work.[115] For example, I/O psychologists have contributed to the design and development of team-based organizations and have developed strategies for designing organizational structures for work flexible enough to ride through turbulent corporate times.

Every I/O psychologist, no matter what their theoretical orientation may be, has some type of lens through which they view an organization's reality. No single theory can adequately explain the full function of human and organizational behavior.[116] The following analogy operationally defines why a multi-perspective psychological paradigm works best to understand human beings within the organizational work environment as the organization is striving to achieve high performance.

> You are placed into a room with absolutely no light; it is black as the darkest night. You are told that there is an object in the room. Your job is to identify the object from where you are located. After a short time, a very narrow beam of light, not very bright, comes on. With this light, not much can be seen. Then, a broader beam of light, still

---

[110] Jewel, L. (1998). *Contemporary industrial/organizational psychology* (3rd ed.). Pacific Grove, CA: Brooks/Cole.

[111] Katzell, R. (1994). Contemporary meta-trends in industrial and organizational psychology. In H. C. Triandis, M. D. Dunnette, & L. M. Hough (Eds.), *Handbook of industrial and organizational psychology* (Vol. 4, pp. 1-89). Palo Alto, CA: Consulting Psychologists.

[112] Muchinsky, P. (2000). *Psychology applied to work: An introduction to industrial and organizational psychology* (6th ed.). Belmont, CA: Wadsworth/Thomson Learning.

[113] Sala, F., & Knight, P. (1995). *Industrial/organizational psychology* (2nd ed.). Pacific Grove, CA: Brooks/Cole.

[114] Rogelberg, S. (Ed). (2002). *Handbook of research methods in Industrial and Organizational Psychology*. Malden, MA: Blackwell.

[115] Landy, F., & Conte, J. (2007). *Work in the 21st Century: An introduction to Industrial and Organizational Psychology* (2nd ed). Malden, MA: Blackwell.

[116] Harrison, M., & Shirom, A. (1999). *Organizational diagnosis and assessment: Bridging theory and practice*. Thousand Oaks, CA: Sage.

not very bright, flips on. Still not much can be seen with the two lights but you begin to make out some type of object in the center of the room. A brighter beam of light now is on; however, because it is an extremely fine beam, it does bounce off the center object but all that you can tell is that something is definitely in the room's center. More and more lights begin to shine on the object. Now, you can tell that it is shiny. A brighter, wider beam of light shines on the object. Because of the light on the object, you can tell that it is black. More light rays begin to shine on the object. You can tell that it is tall, maybe, about two feet. Some of the light beams are broad and some are thin. Some of the shafts of light are bright while some are dim. There are all types of luminosities. After a while, the room begins to lighten up. Finally, the object comes into view. It is the Maltese Falcon.

The Maltese Falcon represents the object of study, which in this particular case is the organizational work environment. The beams of light are synonymous with the different theories and paradigms existing and are attempting to explain the human being in an environment. Individually, each paradigm limits one's acuity of the organizational work environment. However, collectively, the paradigms provide the widest breath of knowledge to provide effectively the best understand of individuals in an organizational work environment.

Because psychology has branched into many different directions, a synergistic, multi-perspective psychological paradigm, an integration of many paradigms, is potentially the most valid process to explore organizational situations. A multi-perspective view as a predictor of organizational high performance is the most valid and permits the widest understanding of how human beings work. With this point kept in mind, a cognitive-behavioral-affective paradigm utilizing a social – humanistic psychological approach is quite effective in explaining and driving toward organizational high performance.

The Biology

Biology is vast and eclectic natural science focused upon the attributes of living organisms.[117] There are at least five foundational principle of today's concept of biology: Cell theory, Evolution, Genetics, Homeostasis, and Energy. Each of these disciplines are analogous of organizations as organizations are considered living organisms.

Exploring each of the foundational principles of biology, cell theory purports cells are the base entity of the structure and functioning of all living organisms.[118]

---

[117] Random House Dictionary (2017). *Biology – Definition*. Retrieved on March 15, 2017, from http://www.dictionary.com/browse/biology?s=t

[118] Random House Dictionary (2017). *Cell Theory – Definition*. Retrieved on March 15, 2017, from http://www.dictionary.com/browse/cell-theory

From an organizational perspective, people are the base entity. Evolution entails any process of formation or growth; however, in regards to biology, it contends a natural selection of the fittest to survive. Organizational evolution purports success and their survival is not guaranteed; subsequently, if an organization is not mutating in some fashion it may become extinct.[119] Genetics is the study of heredity and the attributes of related organisms as they interact with the environment.[120] Organizational genetics refers to the interplay between its internal organizational business model components and its external environment. Homeostasis indicates holistic stability of a living organism through response coordination to stimuli.[121] Organizational homeostasis is the process of obtaining organizational equilibrium when unbalancing forces or tension is introduced consciously (purposely) or unconsciously (accidently) into the organization. Biological energy refers to the capacity of an organism to elicit some level of activity and power internal or external to itself.[122] Organizational energy refers to the level of a system's activity, power, and ability, internal or external to itself, to perform work.

Two other attributes to be explored from the science of biology are the Theory of Systems (also known as General Systems Theory or GST) and the Theory of Complex Adaptive Social Systems. These theories are a natural blend between the sciences of Psychology and Biology.[123] The former attempts to map general principles for how all systems work, especially living systems. Instead of examining phenomena by attempting to break things down into component parts, GST explores phenomena in terms of dynamic patterns of relationship. This shift in focus from things frozen in time to dynamic relationships underlies systems thinking. The latter is an integration of Behavioral and Social Psychology along with the Theory of General and Dynamical Systems with the Theory of Chaos.

As noted, biology is a well-grounded, multi-principle science with a long pedigree with science. Additionally, organizations have a biological component. By understanding the natural science attributes of biology and how it is analogous of organizational biology, insight into how organizations can strive for and subsequently achieve high performance can be realized to a deeper and broader perspective.

---

[119] Random House Dictionary (2017). *Evolution – Definition*. Retrieved on March 15, 2017, from http://www.dictionary.com/browse/evolution?s=t

[120] Random House Dictionary (2017). *Genetics – Definition*. Retrieved on March 15, 2017, from http://www.dictionary.com/browse/genetics?s=t

[121] Random House Dictionary (2017). *Hemostasis – Definition*. Retrieved on March 15, 2017, from http://www.dictionary.com/browse/homeostasis?s=t

[122] Random House Dictionary (2017). *Energy – Definition*. Retrieved on March 15, 2017, from http://www.dictionary.com/browse/energy?s=t

[123] Gell-Mann, M. (1995). Plectics. In John Brockman (Ed.), *The third culture: Beyond the scientific revolution* (pp. 316-332). New York, NY: Simon & Schuster.

The Physics

Physics is the science dealing with matter and energy and their interactions.[124] It is elaborated on further as the universal laws utilized to understand and explain the physical processes and phenomena of a particular system. Physics, one of the most fundamental scientific disciplines, is the natural science involving the study of matter and its motion and behavior through space and time, along with related concepts such as energy and force. Physics plays a vital role in understanding the common world in which everybody engages with every second, every minute, every hour, every day of his or her life. It is race, color, creed, religious, and location bias free because the theories and laws are associated with all living organisms. Physics provides us, in the form of theories and laws, with the best scientific proof possible that a body will move and interact with other bodies in a predictable fashion.

Stephen Hawking's understanding of scientific proof is if you cannot find us wrong, then yes, we could be right![125] Hawking argues there are two requirements for any theory to be true:

1. It must accurately describe a large class of observations based on a model containing only few arbitrary elements.
2. It must make definite predictions about the results of future observations.

According to Hawking, any physical theory is always provisional in the sense it is only a hypothesis and one can never prove it; the hypothesis can only be disproved. Thus, no matter how many times the results of subsequent experiments agree with the theory, one cannot predict whether the next time, the result may not contradict the theory. On the other hand, to disprove a theory, one only has to find a single observation contradicting the theory. Thus, a new theory really is an extension of the previous theory. In practice, a new theory may be devised following add-ons to the previous theory, through modifications or even abandonments. An example is Newton's laws of gravity, which in essence, have been proved not correct by Einstein's predictions. However, since Newton's laws are simple and the difference between its predictions and those of general relativity is very small, Newton's work stands.

The Science

Merriam-Webster defines *science* as knowledge or a system of knowledge covering general truths or the operation of general laws especially as obtained and

---

[124] Merriam-Webster (n.d.). *Physics – Definition*. Retrieved on May 23, 2016, from http://www.merriam-webster.com/dictionary/physics

[125] Hawking, S. (2002). *A brief history of time: From the big bang to black holes*. London, UK: Bantam Press.

tested through scientific method.[126] It is quite common knowledge both psychology and physics are sciences. Merriam-Webster continues with stating a *scientific method* is principles and procedures for the systematic pursuit of knowledge involving the recognition and formulation of a problem, the collection of data through observation and experiment, and the formulation and testing of hypotheses.[127] The Organizational Action Research Schemata following *The Organizational Science* is just such a set of principles and procedures.

The Science of Psychology
Theory of Cognitive Psychology

The first of three psychological concepts effective organizational leaders utilize is cognitive psychology. Cognitive psychology is a theoretical perspective focusing on the realms of human perception, thought, and memory.[128] It portrays people as active processors of information, a metaphor borrowed from the computer world, and assigns critical roles to the knowledge and perspective people bring to their environment. What people do to enrich information, in the view of cognitive psychology, determines the level of understanding they ultimately achieve. According to Matlin,

> Cognitive psychologists generally agree that the birth of cognitive psychology should be listed as 1956… During this prolific year, a large number of researchers published influential books and articles on attention, memory, language, concept formation, and problem solving. Some psychologists even specify a single day on which cognitive psychology was born. On September 11, 1956, many of the important researchers attended a symposium at the Massachusetts Institute of Technology… Enthusiasm for the cognitive approach grew rapidly, so that by about 1960, the methodology, approach and attitudes had changed substantially.[129]

The study of cognitions is considered a dominant approach in psychology today and should be considered a concept both managers and supervisors should be

---

[126] Merriam-Webster (n.d.). *Science – Definition*. Retrieved on February 19, 2017, from https://www.merriam-webster.com/dictionary/science

[127] Merriam-Webster (n.d.). *Scientific Method – Definition*. Retrieved on February 19, 2017, from https://www.merriam-webster.com/dictionary/scientific%20method

[128] Logan, G. (2011). *Cognitive Psychology*. Retrieved on January 30, 2011, from http://www.elsevier.com/wps/find/journaldescription.cws_home/622807/description#description

[129] Matlin, M. (1994). *Cognition*. Fort Worth, TX: Harcourt Brace College Publishers.

aware of and understand.[130] People, employees, are thinking creatures.[131] Employees should be valued for their ability to grasp concepts as well as to understand their duties and responsibilities. Employees can figure out how to do business more effective and be more productive. If managers were to empower their employees, the results may amaze them. The employees' behavior can affect the whole organization.[132]

Within the realm of cognitive psychology, the concept of functionalism is the adaptation of living persons to their environment.[133] Cognitions cannot be properly studied apart from the physical environment in which they take place. Thoughts, feelings, and knowledge can only be understood within the social-cultural context of the organizational work environment.

The cognitive theory has links with the social intelligence behavior theories of Thorndike, David Wechsler included the non-intellective factors of social intelligence and intelligent behavior in his cognitive intelligence discussions.[134] He expressed the concept that intelligence models should include these factors.[135] The interaction between social intelligence and general intelligence were possibly perpetuated from the work of David Wechsler. Additionally, his work potentially evolved into the theories of emotional intelligence. This evolution can be seen in the development of Bar-On's model of the interconnectivity of emotional and social intelligence.[136] He purported this emotional and social intelligence interaction displays how well one knows and expresses themselves in addition how well one knows and relates to others. Therefore, it is how well one can utilize their emotional or affective control to the better good in a social environment. This linkage brings the theoretical orientation to the third psychological concept.

---

[130] Huitt, W. (2003). The information processing approach to cognition. *Educational Psychology Interactive*. Valdosta, GA: Valdosta State University. Retrieved August 16, 2009, from, http://chiron.valdosta.edu/whuitt/col/cogsys/infoproc.html

[131] Larkin, J., & Rainard, B., (2006). A research methodology for studying how people think. *Journal of Research in Science Teaching*, 21(3), 235-254.

[132] Shore, L., Newton, L., & Thornton III, G. (1990). Job and organizational attitudes in relation to employee behavioral intentions. *Journal of Organizational Behavior*, 11(1), 57-67.

[133] James, W. (1890). *The Principles of Psychology*. As presented in Classics in the History of Psychology, an internet resource developed by Christopher D. Green of York University, Toronto, Ontario. Available at http://psychclassics.yorku.ca/James/Principles/prin4.htm

[134] Wechsler, D. (1940). Non-intellective factors in general intelligence. *Psychological Bulletin, 37*, 444-445.

[135] Ibid.

[136] Bar-On, R. (1997). *The Emotional Quotient Inventory (EQ-i): A test of emotional intelligence*. Toronto, Canada: Multi-Health Systems.

Theory of Behavioral Psychology

The second psychological perspective is the behaviorist movement in psychology. It looks toward the use of experimental procedures to study behavior in relation to the environment.

The first behaviorists were Russian. The most famous of the Russian researchers was Ivan Pavlov and his dogs. Pavlovian (or classical) conditioning builds on reflexes: it starts with an unconditioned stimulus and concludes with an unconditioned response -- a reflex! There is then a neutral stimulus associated with the reflex by presenting it with the unconditioned stimulus. After numerous repetitions of this action, the neutral stimulus, alone, will elicit the response. At this point, the neutral stimulus is renamed the conditioned stimulus, and the response is called the conditioned response.

This notion of Stimuli-Response was refined by B. F. Skinner and is perhaps better known as operant conditioning - reinforcing what you want people to do again; ignoring or punishing what you want people to stop doing. Skinner saw human behavior is powerfully shaped by its consequences. Moreover, Skinner felt that psychology was essentially about behavior and that behavior was largely determined by its outcomes.[137] [138]

Edward Lee Thorndike in 1911 established the behaviorist movement in America[139]. When one speaks of Thorndike, cats and "puzzle boxes" immediately jump to one's mind. He utilized cats and puzzle boxes in research animal behaviorism. He formalized two laws of learning because of this research:

1. **The Law of Exercise**: Synonymous with Aristotle's law of frequency. The law states use correlates to strength. Therefore, with this in mind, if an association is utilized often, then the connection between the associations is stronger. Of course, the inverse must also be true. The less it is used, the weaker the connection. These two were referred to as the law of use and disuse respectively.

2. **The Law of Effect**: Related to the law of exercise, if the association is followed by reinforcement, then the connection is strengthened. Likewise, when an association is followed by punishment, it is weakened.

From Thorndike's philosophical perspective, the above two rules can also be true when the operational definition of the term *associations* means communications between people or organizations. Both of these laws are quite

---

[137] Skinner, B. F. (1938). *The Behavior of Organisms*. New York, NY: Appleton-Century-Crofts.
[138] Skinner, B. F. (1953). *Science and human behavior*. New York, NY: Macmillan.
[139] Thorndike, E. (1911). *Animal intelligence: Experimental studies*. New York, NY: Macmillan.

applicable, the law of exercise translates into implying the more often a communication link is used then the stronger it becomes. Obviously, this axiom is true because when people or organizations communicate more; they get to know understand and appreciate each other. As the communication grows, so does the strength of their relationship. The law of effect is then true. As the relationship grows, the two entities enjoy the fruits of their labor as a team. The result of this action is the communication link is further strengthened.

Within the workplace, Thorndike considered successful overt behavior was a result of some construct other than one's intelligence. His school of thought evolved to develop a social intelligence theory associated with behavior.[140]

John B. Watson generally considered the father of behaviorism, argued the inner or unseen experiences, such as cognitions, could not be properly studied, as they were not observable.[141] The implication, from his perspective, was only overt, observable phenomenon should be the purpose of psychological research. Therefore, his career focused upon laboratory experimentation. A stimulus-response model was the end state of his research. From Watson's perspective, a particular stimulus generated each person's response within an environment.

B.F. Skinner further defined the concept of Stimulus-Response.[142] Within Skinner's perspective, he coined the term operant conditioning. Skinner considered operant conditioning as reinforcing what you want people to do again while ignoring or punishing what you want people to stop doing. Skinner believed the consequences of one's actions drove the human behavior train; outcomes determined behavior.[143] A continuance of this school of thought dictated behavior was a valid aspect of psychology.

The concept of behaviorism is one of three psychologically related areas organizational leaders should be cognizant of while developing employees. People do what they do because of what happens to them when they do it. There are three important considerations in behavioral consequences. One is a positive consequence (positive reinforcement) produces an increased rate in the desired behavior. Positive reinforcement strengthens a behavior by providing a consequence an individual finds rewarding. Another consideration is a negative consequence (negative reinforcement). Negative reinforcement is the removal of an unpleasant or an adverse stimulus, which is rewarding to the employee. Negative reinforcement strengthens behavior because it stops or removes an

---

[140] Thorndike, E. (1920). Intelligence and its use. *Harper's Magazine, 140,* 227-235.
[141] Watson, J. (1913). Psychology as the behaviorist views it. *Psychological Review,* 20(2), 158-177.
[142] Skinner, B.F. (1938) The behavior of organisms: An experimental analysis New York, NY: Appleton-Century.
[143] Ibid.

unpleasant experience. The third consideration is punishment. Punishment is the opposite of reinforcement as it is designed to minimize an undesirable response or behavior by applying an aversive stimuli or event. For example, punishment would be to deduct money from a person's paycheck for losing control of equipment; losing equipment is the undesired behavior. By punishing a person in this way, the desired end state is to have the person be more careful and not lose equipment; however, the punishment does not necessarily guide a person to the desired behavior. It can lead to fear, resentment, or aggression.

If a supervisor would like to ensure proper behavior, such as accomplishing tasks ahead of time and under budget, the employee should be reinforced in some fashion meaningful to that employee. This reinforcement may mean a day off to spend more time with their family or take on the form of some type of financial rewards. Either way, the likelihood of the employee repeating tasks ahead of time and under budget is higher because they have learned such behavior will be reinforced.[144] Likewise, it could be concluded, in the development of an organization's emotional intelligence, the employees' behavior toward more resilient, emotional stability probably ought to be reinforced.

Theory of Affective Psychology

In concert with the first two psychological concepts is the affective component of this study's research theoretical orientation. Conceivably, it is also the most applicable element as it refers to the social theory of emotions and because this study dealt with Emotional Intelligence (EI), a term coined by Daniel Goleman.[145] Two researchers of EI, Peter Salovey and John D. Mayer could be consider as leading the charge to understanding emotions from an EI perspective, as they have indicated EI is the ability to control one' emotions.[146] One's emotions have the propensity to cloud cognitive activity thus creating inappropriate or poor behavior.[147] One's ability to control their emotions may play huge dividends in most environments. William James in the 1880's may be one of the first of the classical psychologists to address emotions.[148] James contended one's emotion was a function of how the mind reacted to some type of stimulus in a person's physical

---

[144] Boan, D. (2006). Cognitive-behavior modification and organizational culture. *Consulting Psychology Journal: Practice and Research, 58*(1), 51-61.

[145] Goleman, D. (1995a). *Emotional intelligence*. New York, NY: Bantam Books.

[146] Mayer, J., & Salovey, P. (1997). What is emotional intelligence? In P. Salovey & D. Sluyter (Eds.), *Emotional development and emotional intelligence: Educational implications* (pp. 3-34). New York, NY: Basic Books.

[147] Rosete, D. & Ciarrochi, J. (2005). EI and its relationship to workplace performance outcomes of leadership effectiveness. *Leadership Organizational Development, 26*(5), 388-399

[148] Green, C. (n.d). Classics in the history of psychology: What is an emotion? William James (1884), *Mind*, 9, 188-205. Retrieved on February 20, 2009, from http://psychclassics.yorku.ca/James/emotion.htm

reality. One can observe the interaction of cognitive and behavioral psychological components with affective elements of one's life. All three are definitively inter-related; however, the researcher proposes to understand organizations, one should take the three psychological concepts and tie them to systems theories.

Theory of Social Psychology

Social psychology is the theory through which "to understand and explain how the thoughts, feelings, and behavior of individuals are influenced by the actual, imagined, or implied presence of others."[149] Key to this paradigm is among other personal factors, individuals possess self-beliefs enabling them to exercise a measure of control over their thoughts, actions and feelings, that "what people think, believe, and feel affects how they behave."[150]

Humans are the only species that creates a culture, and every employee develops in the context of the organizational culture in which they work. Cultural norms often serve as the mechanisms through which organizational behaviors are coordinated. They may also regulate conflicts without the intervention of a central, leadership authority.[151] Organizational Culture is the prime determinant of individual development and behavior within an organization.

With the publication of *Social Foundations of Thought and Action: A Social Cognitive Theory*, Albert Bandura determined human functioning was a product of a dynamic interplay of personal, behavioral, and environmental influences.[152] For example, how people interpret the results of their own behavior informs and alters their environments and the personal factors they possess which, in turn, inform and alter subsequent behavior. In general, Bandura believed personal factors in the form of cognition, behavior, affect, and biological events along with the environment influences subsequently creates interactions. From this perspective, a person's behavior is both influenced by and is influencing a person's personal factors and the environment. All variables within a person's system interacts with each other. This leaves credence to an association between cognitive, behavioral, affective approaches with social and humanistic psychology.

---

[149] Allport, A. (1985). The historical background of social psychology. In G. Lindzey & E. Aronson (Eds.), *Handbook of social psychology* (Vol. 1, 3rd ed., pp. 1-46). New York, NY: Random House.
[150] Bandura, A. (1986). *Social foundations of thought and action: A social cognitive theory*. Englewood Cliffs, NJ: Prentice-Hall.
[151] Axelrod, R. (1986). An evolutionary approach to norms. *American Political Science Review*, 80(4), 1095-1111.
[152] Ibid.

Theory of Humanistic Psychology

While behaviorists explain motivation with concepts such as "reward" and "incentive," humanistic interpretations of motivation emphasize such internal sources of motivation as a person's needs for "self-actualization"[153] and the need for "self-determination."[154]

Humanistic psychology is a psychological perspective emphasizing the study of the whole person (Rogers & Freiberg, 1994).[155] Thus, from the humanistic perspective, to motivate means to encourage someone's inner resources-their sense of competence, autonomy, and self-actualization. Cognitive explanations of motivation argue that our behavior is determined by our thinking, not simply by whether we have been rewarded or punished for the behavior in the past. Behavior is initiated and regulated by an individual's plans, goals, beliefs, expectations, and attributions. A central assumption is that people respond not to external events but rather to their interpretation of these events. Social learning theories of motivation take into account both the behaviorists' concern with the outcomes of behavior and the cognitivists' interest in the impact of individual beliefs and expectations. Many influential social learning explanations view motivation as the product of two main forces: the individual's expectation of reaching a goal, and the value of that goal to them. In other words, the important questions are, "If I exert reasonable effort, can I succeed?" and "If I succeed, will the outcome be valuable or rewarding to me?"

Continuing this humanistic perspective, motivation and needs as defined by Abraham Maslow's now famous hierarchy of needs also assists in determining human behavior.[156] Maslow, a behavioral psychologist, is also considered the father of Humanistic Psychology. Humanistic Psychology incorporates aspects of both Behavioral Psychology and Cognitive Psychology. Behaviorists believe that human behavior is controlled by external environmental factors. Cognitive Psychology is based on the idea that internal unconscious forces control human behavior. Maslow rejected the idea that only internal or external forces control human behavior. Instead, Maslow's motivation theory states that man's behavior is controlled by both internal and external factors. In addition, he emphasized that humans have the unique ability to make choices and exercise freewill.

Maslow argued the factors driving or motivating people to act is an ascending scale of needs.[157] Once a group or order of needs is satisfied, the individual will not

---

[153] Maslow, A. H. (1970). *Motivation and personality* (2nd ed.). New York, NY: Harper and Row.
[154] Deci, E., Vallerand, R., Pelletier, L., & Ryan, R. (1991). Motivation and education: The self-determination perspective. *Educational Psychologist*, 26(3&4), 325-346.
[155] Rogers, C., & Freiberg, H. (1994). *Freedom to learn* (3rd ed.). Columbus, OH: Merrill.
[156] Maslow, A. (1970). *Motivation and personality* (2nd ed.). New York, NY: Harper and Row.
[157] Ibid.

be motivated by more of the same, but will seek to satisfy higher order needs. What's more, a higher order need will not be a motivator if lower order needs remain unmet. He laid out five broader layers: the physiological needs, the needs for safety and security, the needs for love and belonging, the needs for esteem, and the need to actualize the self, in that order. The first two layers deals with the basic survival needs of warmth, shelter, and food as well as protection from danger. The last three layers deals with interpersonal relations, self-worth, and realization of potential.

The Science of Biology
Theory of Cells

Through an evolution process initiating with magnifying glasses, the advent of the microscope enabled the discovery and exploration of cells. Though the concept of cells were commonly considered as existing in the mid-1800s, the discovery of cells is commonly given credit to Robert Hooke in the mid-1600s.[158] He happened upon a thin slice of cork and noticed the cork had what resembled the jail cells of the day. The term, cells, has remained with us ever since that day. He since that discovery went on to discover cells were the basic building block of all life.

Cell theory purports cells are the base entity of the structure and functioning of all living organisms.[159] The basics of cell theory indicates:[160]

- Cells are the basic unit of life though not all cells are alike.
- All living organisms are composed of cells.
- Cells arise from pre-exiting cells.
- Energy flow occurs within cells.
- Heredity information (DNA) is passed from cell to cell.
- All cells have the same basic chemical composition.

Within the context of this book, it is not completely important to understand the theory of cells but rather, how the theory of cells is applicable to understanding organizational high performance. A takeaway from the theory of cells is to apply it to the construct of the theory of organizational cells. Upon close examination of an organization, there are a few conclusions drawn, which are:

- People are the organization's basic unit of life though not all people are alike.

---

[158] Science of Aging. (n.d.). *Robert Hooke and the discovery of the* cell. Retrieved on March 20, 2017, from https://www.science-of-aging.com/timelines/hooke-history-cell-discovery.php

[159] Random House Dictionary (2017). *Cell Theory – Definition*. Retrieved on March 15, 2017, from http://www.dictionary.com/browse/cell-theory

[160] ThoughtCo. (n.d.). Cell Theory – Definition. Retrieved on March 20, 2017, from https://www.thoughtco.com/cell-theory-373300

- All organizations are living organisms and are composed of people.
- Organizational energy flow occurs within and between people and its environment.
- Organizational heredity information (Organizational Blueprint; aka Organizational Culture) is passed from person to person.
- All organizations have the same basic composition.

If one is able to put an organization under the proverbial microscope, it is seen people are its most basic unit of life. Because people are complex, adaptive, living organisms, organization are too. People are an organization's most valuable asset through which they are striving to achieve a sustainable advantage or organizational high performance.[161] Individually, people bring their collective blueprint to the organization. An individual blueprint is a blending of all of their past and present attributes defining them. The integration of all the attributes comprising of the individual blueprints as well as how well they function from an interrelationship standpoint creates the organizational blueprint.

Organizational high performance occurs through effective and efficient leadership, development, motivation, and engagement of the people working in them. The more skilled an organization's leaders are in creating an organizational culture where employees feel motivated, the more successful the organization will be. The insight gleamed by studying an organization's inner workings through studying its people, its basic elements will limelight the necessary forces to enable the organization to achieve high performance.

Theory of Evolution

The researcher most associated with the scientific theory of Evolution is perhaps Charles Darwin. Evolution entails any process of formation or growth; however, in regards to biology, it contends a natural selection of the fittest to survive. This contention implies the most powerful or the strongest entity is destined to survive. There is an unspoken component of the theory of evolution. This unspoken component is the theory of evolution is a function of the environment in which the entity exists. The surviving entity is the strongest or most powerful based upon the environment in which it must operate. Therefore, the driving principle of the theory of evolution indicates it is not the strongest nor is it the most powerful, it is not even the most intelligent entity that survives but rather, it is the entities most adaptable to its environment.

---

[161] Harel, H. and Tzafrir, S. (1999). The effects of HRM organizational and market performance of the firm. *Human Resource Management*, 38(3), 185-200.

Organizational evolution purports success and their survival is not guaranteed; subsequently, if an organization is not mutating in some fashion it may become extinct.[162] Organizational extinction means going out of business. Therefore, the greatest mistake an organization can make is to misread both its internal and external environment. Because both environments are in a constant state of flux, the organization must always be learning and thus adapting to ensure its survival.[163] Successful organizational learning enables successful environmental adaptation through constant realignment among the organization's resources and capabilities to most effectively and efficiently work through its Execution Lifecycle, its Market/Customer Lifecycle, and its Product/Services Lifecycle. How well an organization manages this alignment is a function of its core values and goals coupled with its business strategy.

Theory of Genetics

Genetics is the study of heredity as well as how an organism's attributes adjust and interact with its environment.[164] From the word genetics, one can deduce its base word is gene, which is the basic element of heredity. One's heredity is held in their Deoxyribonucleic acid, more commonly known as one's DNA. It is sufficient to know and understand, all living entities have a DNA makeup.

Organizational genetics refers to the smallest of its entities, its organizational DNA and how an organization's internal business model components and its external environment interact. By understanding an organization's genetics, its DNA, if you will, one can understand, at both a macro- and microscopic level, how and why an organization does what it does. The Organizational Action Research Schemata (OAR) is an introspective and interactive exploration of an organization to determine the holist work environment using a scientific methodology. More specifically, OAR explores those attributes potentially inhibiting the organization from achieving its goals and objectives as well as those attributes enabling the organization's success. OAR views firms both broadly, to understand the organizational context, but also microscopically, to gather the facts at the organizational DNA level. An organization's DNA is in essence the architectural blueprint for what makes them be them.

---

[162] Random House Dictionary (2017). *Evolution – Definition*. Retrieved on March 15, 2017, from http://www.dictionary.com/browse/evolution?s=t

[163] Senge, P. (2006). *The fifth discipline: The art and practice of the learning organization* (2nd ed). New York, NY: Random House.

[164] Random House Dictionary (2017). *Genetics – Definition*. Retrieved on March 15, 2017, from http://www.dictionary.com/browse/genetics?s=t

Theory of Homeostasis

Homeostasis indicates holistic stability of a living organism. In general, an organism is content with their environment given the current balancing forces acting on it from its environment.[165] All living organisms strive for stability in their lives. Stability, by some, equates to situational contentment. Given no outside force, the organism will continue with their current path. Without any other input of energy, the organism will not change. It will remain as it is. Not good; not bad, it will exist in just a state of being.

However, with some change in the forces of the organism's environment, with some form of energy input, a sense of conflict is created within the organism. This conflict, a source of pain, for the organism is not desired. The organism will initiate a morphing action to adjust to this new environment so to realize a safe and contented life of existence. This safe and contented life of existence creates a balance of energy and forces for the organism. Once more, the organism is at rest and content with its state of being.

Organizational homeostasis is the process of obtaining organizational equilibrium after unbalancing forces or tensions are introduced consciously (purposely) or unconsciously (accidently) into the organization. This organizational homeostasis equates to the Zeroth Law of Thermodynamics (Thermal Equilibrium) as expressed in the *Science of Physics* section.

Theory of Energy

Biological energy refers to the capacity of an organism to elicit some level of activity and power internal or external to itself.[166] All organisms require a source of energy to exist as well as to continue to live. Alternatively, if an organism does not acquire a certain level of energy, then the outcome is death for the organism. An organism's death is probably not a desired outcome; therefore, for an organism not to die, energy, in the form of food and heat, is necessary.

This biological theory of energy aligns well with the physics of the laws of thermodynamics. The first law of thermodynamics is about the conservation of matter and energy, which purports neither matter nor energy is created or destroyed. Matter is transformed into energy and energy is converted from one form to another. The second law of thermodynamics is concerned with entropy with the implication that without energy an organism will eventually die.

---

[165] Random House Dictionary (2017). *Hemostasis – Definition*. Retrieved on March 15, 2017, from http://www.dictionary.com/browse/homeostasis?s=t

[166] Random House Dictionary (2017). *Energy – Definition*. Retrieved on March 15, 2017, from http://www.dictionary.com/browse/energy?s=t

Organizational energy refers to the level of a system's activity, power, and ability, internal or external to itself, to perform work. An organization, to perform work, requires the energy of its resources. These resources come in the form of people, processes, technology, and financials. These resources are the catalysts to ensure the organization continues to thrive and grow. If these resources stop delivering, then the organization will begin to move toward entropy and ultimately die. Therefore, organizational energy is also associated with the organizational laws of thermodynamics as expressed in the *Science of Physics* section.

Theory of Systems

Systems thinking (also known as General Systems Theory or GST) arose out of the biological sciences.[167] It attempts to map general principles for how all systems work, especially living systems. Instead of examining phenomena by attempting to break things down into component parts, GST explores phenomena in terms of dynamic patterns of relationship. This shift in focus-- from things frozen in time to dynamic relationships-- underlies systems thinking.

What is meant by a "system"? The term "system" can be used for any pattern of relationship, from an atom to a galaxy, from a cell to an ecosystem, from an organ to a human being. A "system" is a collection of things that have relationships among them. As a system, all people function through relationships within and around themselves. Certain patterns of relationship and information flow seem to inhere in all living systems, in plants, animals, ecosystems, social groupings, communities, and organizations. Out of these patterns, our very universe forms itself, and all life within it.

Systems thinking proposed it is the integrating concept of which organizational leaders of all levels should be knowledgeable. So often, an executive often seems focused upon the microcosm of an organization. They may forget each organizational entity is linked to another entity located either internal or external to the organization. Then, this entity is linked to yet another one. The focus of systems thinking is the examination of the whole. It is about the interactions between entities affecting the whole system.[168]

For a given system at a given point of time, only one such state of equilibrium exists if all the forces acting on the system remains constant. An unstable and dynamic system exists because of social disorganization, faulty design, and/or

---

[167] Bertalanffy, L. (1972). The history and status of general systems theory. *The Academy of Management Journal*, 15(4), 407-426.

[168] Appelbaum, E., Bailey, T., Berg, P., & Kalleberg, A. (2001). Do high performance work systems pay off? In L. A. Keister (ed.), *The Transformation of Work (Research in the Sociology of Work, Volume 10)*, (pp.85-107), Bingley, UK: Emerald Group.

organizational malfunctioning or deviancy.[169] However, if there is a change in the forces, then the one such equilibrium state changes.

Within an organization, system-focused thinking explores the dynamics of relationships.[170] The term *system* can be used for any pattern of relationships, from an atom to a galaxy, from a cell to an ecosystem, and from an individual organ to a human being. As a system, all people function through relationships within and around themselves. Human relationships imply information flow. The effectiveness of information flow within an organization can determine the effectiveness of the communications links. To extrapolate, the operational definition of a systems approach, from an industrial/organizational psychologist's perspective, could be the concern with person-environment interactions and the manner by which individuals, groups, and organizations are influenced by this interaction. This definition would then imply organizational leaders should systematically examine the ways individuals interact with other individuals and groups.

Theory of Complex Adaptive Social Systems

The Theory of Complex Adaptive Social Systems is a natural blend between the sciences of Psychology and Biology.[171] Namely, a integration of Behavioral and Social Psychology along with the Theory of General and Dynamical Systems with the Theory of Chaos.

A complex entity indicates a wide breadth of variance between its elements; it is merely a system of independent but interacting elements whose outcomes must be examined as a whole as opposed to individual interactions. Being an adaptive entity implies an ability to adjust or alter itself; in essence, the entity learns from its environment. An entity is social when an arrangement of relationships exists between and among the elements comprising the entity. A system exists when an entity contains a collection of interconnected and dependent elements.

With the above definitions, one easily can conclude an organization is a complex adaptive social system. Breaking down this systemic description, organizations are:

---

[169] Young, T. (1991). Chaos and social change: Metaphysics of the postmodern. *Social Science Journal*, 28(3), 289-305.

[170] Wittmann, W., & Hattrup, K. (2004). The relationship between performance in dynamic systems and intelligence. *Systems Research and Behavioral Science*, 21(4), 393–409.

[171] Gell-Mann, M. (1995). Plectics. In John Brockman (Ed.), *The third culture: Beyond the scientific revolution* (pp. 316-332). New York, NY: Simon & Schuster.

- **Complex**: An organization is comprised of individuals, dyads, teams, groups, sections, and offices. They utilize technology, governance, and processes to define the what, where, when, why, and how they collectively operate. Each of these organizational elements are interrelated and dependent upon each other for survival.
- **Adaptive**: An organization is influenced by and change accordingly to the internal and external environmental forces acting on them.
- **Social**: An organization is comprised of people as its basic core element. Its associated people, both internal and external to the organization, form relationships and communicate with each other.
- **System**: An organization is an assembly of elements, which are individuals, dyads, teams, groups, sections, and offices brought together to accomplish a mission through achieving goals and objectives. From a Gestalt perspective, they operate as one or as a whole as opposed to individual components.

From a behavioral and social psychology perspective, human systems strive to achieve a state of equilibrium, very similar to the concept present in the Science of Physics and the Zeroth Law of Thermodynamics (Thermal Equilibrium).

For an organization, a Complex Adaptive Social System is a collection of individual, human systems or elements interconnected in a hierarchical organizational structure. A complex adaptive system of humans has the capability for self-organization. This self-organization is defined as a methodology through which an organizational structure develops in an open system.[172] This methodology moves the organization from chaotic, disorganized, undifferentiated, and independent states to organized as well as highly differentiated and interdependent states.[173] These concepts of self-organization emerged from the works of Prigogine's work on equilibrium thermodynamics and Haken's theory of Synergetic.[174] [175] [176] [177] [178]

---

[172] Barton, S. (1994). Chaos, self-organization, and psychology. *American Psychologist*, 49(1), 5-14.

[173] Farmer, J. (1995). The second law of organization. In John Brockman (Ed.), *The third culture: Beyond the scientific revolution* (pp. 359-375). New York, NY: Simon & Schuster.

[174] Haken, H. (1983). *Advanced synergetics: Instability hierarchies of self-organizing systems and devices*. Berlin, Germany: Springer-Verlag.

[175] Haken, H. (1988). *Information and self-organization: A macroscopic approach to complex systems*. Berlin, Germany: Springer-Verlag.

[176] Nicolis, G., & Prigogine, I. (1977). *Self-organization in non-equilibrium systems*. New York, NY: John Wiley.

[177] Nicolis, G., & Prigogine, I. (1989). *Exploring complexity*. New York, NY: W. H. Freeman.

[178] Prigogine, I., & Stengers, I. (1984). *Order out of chaos: Man's new dialogue with nature*. New York, NY: Bantam Books.

These human elements comprising organizations operate autonomously and can respond independently to local situations. These individual elements gather information from and provide information to other elements according to the rules, policies, laws, and culture of the environment both internal and external to the organization. Optimally, they enable the organization to grow as a function of time. However, there can be and often is competition between the individual human elements as well as between the larger elements, such as teams, offices, and divisions. All of these elements, no matter at what level, are vying for recognition and empowerment over the other elements. While competition can be beneficial, it can also be destructive.

Researchers of complexity have determined with an organizational system both randomness and determinism may coexist. These researchers are concluding the organization cannot always be understood by reducing it to its basic or simpler parts. To do so, one may note instability is commonplace and change is frequently abrupt and discontinuous.[179] Therefore, the key is looking at an organization as a complex adaptive social system. To have this view provides critical understanding into the totality of its functional inner workings as the organization strives forward to high performance.

Theory of Neuroscience

Merriam-Webster defines neuroscience as a branch of the life sciences dealing with the brain and the biology of human thoughts, behaviors, and emotions. It is amazing, the human brain, weighing in at about three pounds, is possibly the most powerful and complex living organ. Perhaps, it must have to be to accomplish its mission in life, which is to control all aspects of the human body. To accomplish its mission, the brain has over 100 billion nerve cells, which are born, grow, and connect. The brain controls heart rates, emotions, memory, language, and appetite. It develops and shapes our thoughts, beliefs, hopes, dreams, and imaginations.

Thinking about the brain, it is normally associated with being a supercomputer. However, unlike any current computer, the brain seems to have an unlimited storage capacity. If one relates it to a social network, the brain has far more network connections of any social network. Lastly, as a tool, the brain has enabled humans to consider and then achieve huge undertakings, such as going to the moon and safely returning back to earth, making art, creating literature, and composing music as well as many more breathtaking endeavors in-between.

Linking the brain and the individual, the brain protects the individual. Its survival mechanism is the dialectic nature of threat and reward. It is because of the reticular

---

[179] Casti, J. (1994). *Complexification: Explaining a paradoxical world through the science of surprise*. New York, NY: Harper Collins.

brain's individual survival instincts, employees will initially fear any type of leader's decisional concepts focused on achieving organizational goals and transformational initiatives. Employees will normally consider the leader's decisions as self-serving and thus not in the best interest of the employee.

A person's Reticular Brain, focused on individual survival, desires to avoid individual survival threats and to seek out or to approach the reinforcing nature of rewards. One may say these two actions are the primary responses of the reticular brain. It literally is one or the other; there is no in-between.

Because the reticular brain is focused on the overall best interest of the employee in an either/or scenario, the leader must transmit in their conversations, behaviors, and emotions that the employee is ok or good not bad. Also, the leader must indicate the employee is making right decisions based upon what they understand about the situation not wrong ones; the employee is or being successful and not a failure; and the employee is enabled to be in and not out of the moment. Lastly, the leader is a friend as opposed to a foe.

The bilateral aspect of the reticular brain, avoidance and approach are invariably linked to the social nature of human beings. A trigger within an organizational setting is the leader's decisional concepts focused on achieving organizational goals and transformational initiatives. Though not mentioned earlier, the organizational trigger is also an employee's peers. Peers' thoughts, behaviors, and emotions can trigger one or the other bilateral responses of the reticular brain. Therefore, any social interaction has the possibility of eliciting a reticular brain bilateral response of avoidance or approach. This means, respectively, a person may be defensive and resistive or be collaborative and supportive.

From a leadership perspective and with their decisional concepts focused on achieving organizational goals and transformational initiatives, the leader wants to accomplish two actions. First, they want to minimize the employee's view of there being a threat resulting in defensive and resistive thoughts, behaviors, and emotions. Second, they want to maximize the employee's view of there being rewards associated with the leader's decisions resulting in collaborative and supportive thoughts, behaviors, and emotions.

To understand the concept of these two actions, when a person is experiencing anxiety, distrust, stress, their reticular brain is stimulating its defensive circuits signifying a threat. The results of this state is more resources are spent on the individual's defense and survival and less resources on the desirable thoughts, behaviors, and emotions focused on such activities as, but not limited to, effective communications, innovation, productivity, team work, and concentration.

However, when a person is not experiencing anxiety and stress and is working in a trusting environment whereas the leader is portraying such activities as engagement and behavioral reinforcement, then a more conducive work environment exists. At this point, the person is working beyond his or her reticular brain and probably on into his or her limbic brain and cerebral cortex. As such, the person is experiencing commitment with a higher level of connection with the leader as well as with the organization. This commitment and connection exists because the cerebral cortex's pre-frontal lobe is producing dopamine, which is the reward neurotransmitter. With the production of dopamine comes an increase of the person's emotional, memory, and cognitive capabilities.

At the end of the day, leaders make decisions designed to achieve the organization's goals, which in turn enable mission achievement. Leaders are concerned with developing and constantly improving the holistic organizational environment, both internally and externally. Last, leaders are focused on results. Leaders, who understand the neuroscience of leadership, will understand how to best approach employees regarding decisional concepts focused on achieving organizational goals and transformational initiatives. Having an understanding of the neuroscience of leadership and knowing how the brain actually works enable the leader to create effectively a high performing organizational work environment and employees who are, themselves, high performers.

Neuroscience of Leadership

As mentioned, neuroscience is the scientific study of the brain and nervous system. It is a multidisciplinary branch of biology and focuses on the human anatomy, biochemistry, molecular biology, and physiology of neurons and neural circuits.

The U.S. Army Field Manual (FM) 6-22, defines leadership as "the process of influencing people by providing purpose, direction, and motivation while operating to accomplish the mission and improve the organization."

Kimberly Schaufenbuel, program director of UNC Executive Development, stated neuroscience provides the link between human interaction and effective leadership practices. The neuroscience of leadership focuses on utilizing neuroscience concepts to such areas as leadership and its development, management and its training as well as the application of both leadership and management practices to achieve successfully organizational goals and transformational initiatives. The neuroscience of leadership provides a vast array of tools through which to empower an organization as well as its employees to not only strive but also to achieve high performance. Neuroscience applied in realm of organizational leadership creates an environment of communication, inspiration, innovation, motivation, collaboration as well as mission and goal achievement.

The Brain

Paul D. MacLean, an American physician and neuroscientist, as part of his triune brain theory, postulated the human brain has evolved into three components with more recent components developing at the top and front of the brain. MacLean's concept of the brain components states a person has three physical brain systems with unique functions. MacLean's components are:

Survival Brain System

The archi-pallium or primitive (Reticular) brain, comprising the structures of the brain stem - medulla, pons, cerebellum, mesencephalon, the oldest basal nuclei - the globus pallidus and the olfactory bulbs. Some people call this system the reptilian brain, which refers to those brain structures related to territoriality, ritual behavior and other reptile behaviors.

The reticular brain system's focus is avoiding pain; therefore, it is focused on survival of the individual more than it is with gaining pleasure. It stores a person's instinct and survival mechanisms incorporated from very early primal evolutionary processes. This area is what makes immediate decisions. It holds fast to immediate reflexive behaviors and responses used throughout everyday life toward that survival end state. It stores the physical actions keeping the brain and the individual consistently in balance with their environment.

Leader' decisions are, quite often, first looked upon as begin either a threat or not a threat to the individual. Remembering the default setting, if the initial and immediate thought is the decision is a threat to the individual, then the reticular brain will immediate go into flight or fight mode with thoughts, behaviors, and emotional responses focused on individual survival.

Leaders, to leverage the strengths of the reticular brain system, must create a conversation leading to the employee reaching an immediate decision and concluding the moment, the leader-employee relationship, is necessary for their survival. Since it is strictly responsible for its own survival, the employee's reticular brain will be more likely to be attentive if they are talking about its favorite subject: itself. Within seconds, the reticular brain wants to know what the plan is for their immediate survival. If the conversation is proven worthy of attention, then and only then, will the other parts of the brain get involved.

In essence, the conversation must take on a primal survival perspective. The reticular brain only understands a few words at most. The optic nerve goes directly to the reticular brain, and so it is influenced primarily by visual images. Since the reticular area is the rest of the brain's attention gatekeeper, this means the leader must be more visually creative with how to communicate in order to persuade the reticular portion to invest the rest of the brain's energy. Therefore, visioning and visually stimulating "what if" questions will relate well with the reticular brain.

Contrast is understood by the reticular brain extremely easily. Easily understood conversations will be more likely to be rewarded with attention. It will also speed up the decision making process. Showing contrast by the employee demonstrating before and after; showing the pain and relief from the pain. Showing why the employee will be better is significant.

The conversation may also include tapping into the employee's pain points, appealing to their innate selfishness, demonstrating importance through contrast, emphasizing value tangibility, focusing on beginning and ending, and using visual metaphors. If the reticular brain deems the leader's decisions as not a threat, it allows the leader's decisional concepts to pass onward to his or her Limbic (emotional) brain. By striking up an emotional chord of survival, the reticular brain system will engage the emotional, Limbic Brain System.

Emotional Brain System

The paleo-pallium or intermediate (old mammalian) brain, comprising the structures of the limbic system. The Limbic Brain refers to those brain structures, wherever located, associated with social and nurturing behaviors, mutual reciprocity, and other behaviors and affects that arose during the age of the mammals.

The Limbic Brain, the second to the oldest portion of the human brain. Brain research purports the emotional brain chooses one's actions based on memories and emotions, long before the thinking brain gets involved. It is for this reason why many people find it difficult to follow through with their resolutions to change a behavior. Therefore, a starting point is to utilize techniques enabling employees to leverage their emotional brain and its involuntary responses to work for, rather than against, their best interest.

Emotional regulation is critical for effective decision-making and action in complex and constantly changing environments. To best connect to an employee's limbic, emotional brain, the leader should use emotionally charged language to enable employee's perceptions on, thoughts about, interactions with, and emotions about their environment to change. This connection level will directly address the areas of the brain where unprocessed emotions and memories block the employee from achieving and thus lead the employee to using his/her logical, cerebral brain system.

Logical Brain System

The neo-pallium, also known as the superior or rational (new mammalian) brain, comprises almost the whole of the hemispheres (made up of a more recent type of cortex, called neocortex) and some subcortical neuronal groups. The Cerebral Cortex, also known as the Neocortex represents that cluster of brain structures involved in advanced cognition, including planning, modeling and simulation.

Cerebral Cortex, the youngest portion of the human brain. To best connect with and subsequently access and influence the cerebral brain, the logical part of the brain, the leader should use the language of logic. The cerebral brain processes the written language and is responsible for complex thinking, calculating, and rationalizing decisions.

The cerebral brain operates in a serial fashion. If information is presented too quickly, because the cerebral brain uses many resources, it can become overloaded. A leader understanding the interworking of the cerebral brain creates a conversation designed to provide information in small, logically linked bites to the employee. This conversation has the leader asking questions as well as clarifying and giving feedback in a succinct and specific ways. The words a leader uses would be simple, relevant to employee's background, and thus easy for the employee to understand. A leader's conversation facilitating an employee's thinking, recollection, and decision-making to unleash his/her cerebral, logical brain's potential will enable the employee to move forward in their solution-focused, action-oriented journey toward their desired, future state.

Understanding the functionality of the brain and leveraging this understanding in transformational initiatives will more completely meet, if not exceeded, the requirements in the demanding and fast-paced environment that currently exists. The interaction between the brain and one's environment relates to the inherent connection of living within a community. A person cannot survive alone in the world without other people. The complex internal essence and connections toward the self and others are the main key to how the complex circuitry of neurons, known as the brain, coexist with outside forces. Direct integration of the holistic brain system and using all of the brain's processing mechanisms will have the greatest level of employee success. Additionally, executives and other professionals boost can their productivity, improve their resilience to stress, and increase their sense of self-confidence to perform with poise in presentations and negotiations.

The Brain Hormones (Neurotransmitters)

The brain is a complex organ and integral to the human being's existence. The brain is responsible for integrating a person's thoughts, behaviors, and emotions. Linked to this integration is the chemicals created by the brain, which falls under the term called neurotransmitters. The brain generates many neurotransmitters. Not to belittle all the other neurotransmitters; however, there are five playing critical roles in the life of the human being. These five neurotransmitters are Endorphin, Dopamine, Serotonin, Oxytocin, and Cortisol.

Endorphin

Endorphin help people overcome stress and pain caused due to physical activities. The production of endorphin enables the long distance runner to keep on going when they are hurting. In addition, it helps with injury recovery and improves one's immunity as well. Humor and laughter also helps create endorphin. Perhaps, it is for this reason the saying, laughing is good for the soul, actually exists.

The majority of a person's emotions and memories are processed by limbic system of the brain. The limbic system includes the hypothalamus, which is responsible for a range of functions from breathing and sexual satisfaction to hunger and emotional response. The hypothalamus is the command-and-control center of a person's endocrine system and decides, among other functions, when to eat, when to begin puberty, and when endorphins are needed. It is connected to a person's central nervous system and releases hormones to the body when it detects adjustments are necessary.

Endorphin is released when the body is in pain or in stress. Endorphins may be associated with increased levels of rage or anxiety. If a person's endorphins overdo their job or the hypothalamus misinterprets the endorphin cue, a person could be flooded with fight-or-flight hormones at the slightest hint of trouble or worry.

Endorphin are sometimes described as the body's naturally induced chemical to help the body feel good. To achieve a good feeling, they interact with the receptors in your brain reducing your perception of pain. In other words, endorphins act as analgesics. Therefore, in the absence of pain, the body can have a euphoric feeling as well as feeling focused and assists in mood improvement.

This euphoric feeling can be enhanced through exercising, which is one method through which you can induce the body to release endorphins. Laughing is also found to release endorphins; it is for this reason people may laugh nervously when in stressful or tense situations. Physical touching, such in the form of a handshake, has a propensity of producing endorphins too.

Associated conceptually with touching, when a person is touching others by finding a common purpose and working together to achieve results has the same propensity of inducing endorphins. Unrealized accomplishments or the lack of recognition leads to the exact opposite of employee satisfaction, which is employee frustration. This employee frustration leads to dissatisfied and disengaged employees. So, how often do your employees experience a sense of accomplishment?

Dopamine

Dopamine is considered the feel good neurotransmitter or hormone. It is tied to motivation and enjoyment. Dopamine is responsible for the feelings experienced with you win a prize, meet a goal, and eat your favorite meal or dessert. Unfortunately, cannabis or marijuana will also empower a person's brain to create or release an overage of dopamine. People will say they or someone is addicted to a drug; however, it is not the drug, per se, to which they are addicted. They are actually addicted to what the brain produces because of the drug. The person is addicted to dopamine.

On a similar note, dopamine is produced when people talk about themselves. Remembering the addictive nature of dopamine, if a person is thought of only wanting to talk about them self, it is because they have become addicted to the dopamine created. Therefore, when a person just wants to talk about them self, it is because their brain is releasing dopamine and it is for this reason they want to continue talking about them self.

Dopamine is associated with stimulus and reward/pleasure along with the concept of learning how to increase or find more stimuli to increase their reward/pleasure sensations. Dopamine is often called the brain's pleasure chemical. However, perhaps more accurately it is associated with the pleasure associated with desire and anticipation.

Desire and anticipation is pleasurable because these feelings elicit thoughts about a possible reward. This reward can come in many forms; it can be a physical reward or more aligned to a virtual reward. For example, think back to perhaps your first date or your first job. What was going through your mind? The anticipation could bring feelings of nervousness. The nervousness could be a conflict between the stress hormone called cortisol and the love hormone called oxytocin both of which are presented next. However, you might have had feelings of anticipatory pleasure. This anticipatory pleasure is because of dopamine was being released by your brain.

So, dopamine aids in controlling a person's sense of reward and pleasure within their brain and, in particular, with the expectation of a reward. Additionally, it aids in regulating movement and emotional responses. When combining its association with reward, pleasure, movement, and emotional responses, it not only permits us in recognizing rewards but also empowers us to move toward the objects giving us a reward and pleasure. The more often the reward and pleasure sensation is realized then the more often people will seek it out with an ever increasing expectation of continued rewards.

Think about the concept of dopamine toward organizational and individual high performance from a leadership perspective. Employees seek reward and pleasure sensations. How often do you provide a dopamine surge to your employees in the form of rewarding them or being a catalyst for a pleasurable sensation?

If a leader leverages their knowledge about dopamine, then an employee's biological need for dopamine can be used to empower employees to achieve high performance. This individual high performance perspective subsequently leads to organizational high performance. Leveraging this biological need for dopamine can come in the form of positive reinforcement and recognition through engaging with and encouraging employees.

As a leader, you can infuse your employees with their desired dopamine surge through several activities. Praise sincerely your employees in a timely fashion, such as immediately after their behavior reflects desirable traits or outcomes. Additionally, during this praise, be specific as to what the employee did to receive the accolades and recognition. This specificity should be as precise and obvious as you can be. You should lay it out so it removes all doubt as to what the employee did and how it reflects not only on the employee but also on their team and the organization. Lastly, instill a quantifiable element to your accolade and recognition for the employee; this point depicts the level of your attention. This quality accolade and recognition will invariably increase the employee's dopamine level. Additionally, it will entice the employee to seek it out more readily by repeating the appropriate behavior and achieving the desirable outcome. The employee will definitely keep it in mind for his/her projects moving forward.

Serotonin

Serotonin is considered the feel good neurotransmitter or hormone. As such, it is involved in the brain's association with mood and emotions to thoughts, memories, and perceptions. Specifically, the serotonin released in the pre-frontal portion of the cerebral cortex regulates thoughts, memory, and perceptions. Serotonin the hippocampus regulates memory and mood. Lastly, serotonin in other limbic brain areas, such as the amygdala, also regulates mood.

Serotonin has a regulatory or balancing activity centered on how a person lives and recollects their life. Therefore, one probably can easily see its mood and emotion linkages to the challenging feelings of depression, aggression, panic attacks, and anxiety. How a person remembers a past event from a mood or emotional perspective can determine how a person feels or perceives a current event and how the person reacts because of it.

Serotonin is also associated with feelings of self-confidence, significance, pride, and status. It creates in people the ambition for recognition by our supervisors and our peers. Additionally, it is an enabler to relationship building, which is synonymous with team building. High levels of serotonin have been found in people considered open, clear-minded, and focused as well as socially dominant personality types.

Simon Sinek, in his book, *Leaders Eat Last: Why Some Teams Pull Together and Others Don't* calls serotonin the leadership chemical and it is necessary for the creation of team allegiance and cohesion. Simon Sinek also argues people are mentally wired to submit to organizational hierarchy. Therefore, leaders can elicit cooperation, trust and change within their organization and with employees. However, when leaders betray the employees' trust, employees become distrustful and subsequently disengaged.

Oxytocin

Oxytocin, also known as the love hormone, exists to empower a person to overcome stress and anxiety. However, as will be noted, oxytocin is a double-edged sword.

Oxytocin enhances a person's feelings of trust and personal emotional bonding as well as feelings of social connectivity. However, even with the above sentences stated, oxytocin is also considered or linked to enhancing fear emotions or psychological pain as presented in the next section on cortisol. Therefore, aligned with this thought, if a person experiences some level of social defeat, oxytocin reinforces this experience.

Oxytocin is found to perhaps enhance the positive while also enhancing the negative spectrum of human emotions. It can either fortify relationship bonds but it is also associated with feelings of social isolation and loneliness. Understanding the duality of oxytocin, a leader can be focused on creating positive bonding relationships enhanced by oxytocin while minimizing the attributes of poor relationship building.

Cortisol

The cortisol-stress hormone and the oxytocin-love hormone actually work together creating a deep-rooted fear-based memory during, and after, times of distress. Cortisol is dangerous to a person's wellbeing if it remains in his or her system for a long time. It begins to breakdown the non-essential bodily organs and tissues so to maintain the high glucose levels necessary for the survival of the vital organs.

The cortisol-stress hormone is known to cause a wide variety of common human challenges. High blood pressure, heart disease, high anxiety, and depression are associated with stress. Additionally, stress is associated with weight gain, immunity issues, both mental and physical fatigue, and emotional outbursts, such as road rage.

It thought this combination of cortisol and oxytocin is linked to the reticular brain's survival mechanism so a person will vividly recall life-threatening situations so to not repeat them. In essence, the hormonal combination flags the traumatic experience evoking fear and flags the memory as important.

Neuroscience of Organizational Change

In an article, copied here, the *TMI Journal 2013* indicates Walter McFarland[180] thoughts on change. He described how neuroscience research increases knowledge of the brain and may be a source of new insight into the theory and practice of organizational change. Walter shared insights on specific attributes of the brain that inform behavior during organizational change, how current change approaches actually trigger resistance in the brain, and how key neuroscience-informed actions can improve performance of change activities.

It is vital to the success of Change Practitioners to understand two of these hard-wired systems involved in fight/flight reactions—*error detection* and *fear response*.

We now know human behavior in the workplace does not work as we had thought. We have learned that evolutionary processes affect how the brain relates to Change. Five things about the brain can help Change Practitioners increase their effectiveness:

1. **The brain focuses on *surviving*** – in physical, social, and organizational contexts.
2. **The brain develops specialized survival systems**, involving motivation, memory, error detection, and fear response. All of these systems, which have evolved over eons, operate in today's organizational environment. *Wanting* something is driven by the dopaminergic system; *avoiding* or flight response is driven by serotonin. Most importantly for those of us who help in Organization Development, *the motivation to* avoid is stronger than that to approach.

---

[180] Walter McFarland is 2013 Board Chair of the American Society for Training and Development (ASTD), the world's largest professional association dedicated to the training and development profession. He was a senior vice president at Booz Allen Hamilton where he led the firm's Global Human Capital and Learning businesses; and a senior principal at Hay Management Consultants, where his business focus was human capital, learning, and change.

3. **The brain "hardwires" patterns of thinking.** The brain developed hardwired neural systems for surviving and navigating the external environment. Working memory (understand, decide, recall, memorize, inhibit), is located in the prefrontal cortex; and habit memory (patterns of behavior), is located in the basal ganglia. "Error signals" can trigger an amygdala hijack, which overwhelms working memory and creates a profound fear response and resistance to Change. In the organizational context, habits are good—they create efficiencies during normal operations; or bad—they can be very difficult and painful to change.
4. **The brain can be "rewired."** Neuroplasticity is becoming more and more important in this work. Helping people "think better" is an emerging leadership competency.
5. **"Bad is stronger than good."**

Summary—Five Things About the Brain	
Five Things About the Brain	**Implications for Change Practitioners**
• It focuses on surviving	• Change can threaten survival
• It evolves specialized systems	• Change affects multiple brain systems; *Change is pain.*
• It "hardwires"	• Change demands changing habits
• It can be "rewired"	• Neuroplasticity can be learned
• "Bad is stronger than good"	• Change efforts focus on the positive

Imagine a new kind of organization optimized for Change—an organization that uses Change as fuel to become continuously better and more competitive. In such an organization, Change is no longer something it does, but something it is.

Here is a neuroscience-based Change framework for organizations:

1. **Integrate Change into strategy.** He suggests that leaders link Change to the organization's destiny by declaring the importance of Change in the context of strategy, giving Change powerful context and purpose. This linkage reduces organizational anxiety about Change and sets the stage for creating a "Change focused culture." Linking Change to strategy connects the dots for people.
2. **Shape the *external* environment.** Meet external change head-on by using robust environmental scanning and futures techniques to better anticipate and shape market changes. Reduce organizational anxiety and fatigue from endlessly *following* market changes. Motivate staff to think about Change proactively and constructively. Avoid being a fast follower of changes driven by others.

3. **Shape the *internal* environment.** Make the organization a place for great thinking. Integrate Change into day-to-day business by vesting responsibility for Change in the local line people. Focus senior management on game-changing opportunities and create a brain-friendly environment.
4. **Create a change-enabled workforce.** Identify, brand, and assess Change-related competencies in the organization. Organization leaders help others think better about Change.
5. **Continuously generate and celebrate short and long-term wins.** The key is fighting *bad* through recurring experiences with *good*. Neuroscience research affirms the importance of celebration in best thinking. Short-term celebration should occur immediately after success. Long-term celebration should be tied to major milestones. Celebration helps the brain rewire Change as "wanting."

In summary, McFarland showed the field of organizational change has been growing and learning across its sixty-six-year history. Understanding the brain adds real insight into more effective Change leadership, better engaging people in Change, and building organizations better at Changing.

The Science of Physics
Theory of Dynamical Systems

The Theory of Dynamical Systems has its roots in mathematics and Classical Mechanics. It is utilized in understanding the behavior of complex dynamical systems. Complex organizations, as defined earlier, are those holistic entities comprised of elements interrelated and dependent upon each other. A dynamical system is a system having a point's location being dependent upon time, which can be explained by a function.

Time can be either discrete or continuous. Discrete time is viewed as distinct points, such as those displayed by a digital clock (i.e. it is first 10:25 then 10:26 then 10:27). Continuous time is reflected in the concept that time is divided into infinitesimally short periods between points of time, such as viewed by an analog clock with a sweeping second hand.

A function is a process with an input and a subsequent output; so, for any specific input, there is a specific output. One type of dynamical system function is captured by the evolution rule, which describes what a system's future state will be from a specific current state. The evolution rule function describes systems in terms of being either stochastic or deterministic, equating respectively to chaotic verses non-chaotic dynamics.

A stochastic, chaotic system is one whereas an event within the system may affect the evolution of the future state. There is seemingly randomness of the future state. Tracking the future state of the stock market, after the fact, is an example of a stochastic system. Of course, probability theory, utilized by stock portfolio managers, attempts to predict the future state.

If the evolution rule function describes a system as deterministic or non-chaotic, it is saying given a specific amount of time and current state and then only one future state can follow. For example, if you put meat into a meat grinder, you will always get that specific meat to come out but in a ground state. There is no randomness. Essentially, the evolution rule of the Dynamical Systems Theory states a system, such as an organization, adapts/changes/evolves as a function of time.

Theory of Chaos

Chaos theory focuses on the behavior of dynamical systems. As a dynamical system, the theory of chaos indicates small changes in the organization's initial state can create a wide range of outcomes. The challenge is, of course, one only knows what one knows of the system's current state. Therefore, the accuracy of the system's future state is a function of how precise the knowledge is of its current state.

A chaotic system seemingly is considered as not having any patterns; its activities seem purely random. However, in reality, there are patterns and feedback loops as well as forces acting throughout the system. The chaos theory takes a perspective of deterministic systems, in that, a system's future state can be predicted if the current state is accurately known.

An organizational system can be considered a chaotic system because there are forces in play, internally and externally, throughout the organization. These forces create the social and environmental pressures creating the catalyst for an organization to need to adapt. Whether the need or pressure is enough to cause the organization to adapt is yet to be determined. The key to leveraging the chaos theory to achieve organizational high performance is to utilize small and discrete steps. These steps are:

- Determine the organization's current state, as accurately as possible
- Determine the organization's desired future state
- Conduct a Gap Analysis between the current and the desired future state
- Move onward and forward in a journey toward the organization's desired future state in small and discrete steps

An organization can achieve high performance through the effective and efficient use of these steps associated with the chaos theory.

Theory of Classical Mechanics

Classical mechanics is commonly called Newtonian Mechanics because of the system of physics started by Sir Isaac Newton in the beginnings of the 20th Century. Classical mechanics is focused on the laws of physics concerned with motion, more specifically, describing how forces influence the motion or behavior of entities. The forces are push or pull actions on a body having a tendency to move it in the action's direction. However, to realize this tendency, the force's characteristics, magnitude, direction, and point of application, must be appropriate. The laws of physics are the three laws of motion, which were written about by Sir Isaac Newton in the "Principia Mathematica Philosophiae Naturalis" in 1686.

These three laws of Classical Mechanics describe the physics of inertia, acceleration, and reaction, which, in turn, have application in the attributes of organizational performance. The first law of motion is sometimes referred to as the law of inertia, which is a body's resistance to change its current state, be it at rest or in motion. This law, as will be note in all of the laws of motion, has a direction (vector) component to it. However, for this fundamental level, it is only necessary to understand directions (vectors) exist but not necessary to understand how direction (vectors) come into play. Inertia directly correlates to a body's mass; therefore, the greater a body's mass, the greater its inertia.

The first law of motion/inertia states:

> An object at rest will remain at rest unless an outside force acts on it,
> and an object in motion at a constant velocity will remain in motion
> in a straight line unless acted upon by an outside force.[181]

Therefore, this law is stating an object has a tendency to stay in its current state, be it at rest or in motion. Remember, the reason why an object does or does not keep on going, even when there seems to be no outside force acting on the object, is because of the ever-present friction. Friction is the force between a body in motion and the surface on which it moves. It is the external force acting on an object, which causes it to slow down when no other external force acts upon it.[182]

From an organizational performance perspective, the first law of organizational motion, which does have a direction (vector) component to it, states:

---

[181] Hodanbosi, C. (1996). *The first and second laws of motion*. Edited by Jonathan G. Fairman. Retrieved on August 4, 2016, from https://www.grc.nasa.gov/www/k-2/WindTunnel/Activities/first2nd_lawsf_motion.html

[182] Boundless (2016). *The first law: Inertia*. Boundless Physics. Boundless, Retrieved 04 Aug. 2016 from https://www.boundless.com/physics/textbooks/boundless-physics-textbook/the-laws-of-motion-4/newton-s-laws-46/the-first-law-inertia-236-10947/

An organization's tendency is to maintain its status quo in how it thinks, behaves, and reacts unless a force, either internal or external, acts on it.

As with Newton's first law of motion/inertia, an organization's inertia is its resistance to change from its current state to a future state. Additionally, its inertia correlates to the organization's mass.

The second law of motion states:

If an unbalanced force acts on an object, the object will experience acceleration (or deceleration), that is, a change of speed.[183]

This second law of motion, which does have a direction (vector) component to it, indicates an object will require a net sum of forces to stop or slow it down, to get it moving or speed it up, or to change its direction. If the net sum of forces is negative, the object will slow down or go in one direction. Conversely, if the net sum of forces is positive, the object will speed up or go in the other direction. The generalized, without a direction (vector) component, formula associated with the second law of motion is:

$$F = ma$$

Whereas:

    F = the net sum of the forces acting on an object

    m = the object's mass; how much matter it contains

    a = the acceleration the force causes; it is how an object's velocity changes over time

If the object is moving at a constant velocity (speed) and in a straight line, the following formula is applicable:

$$d = vt$$

Whereas:

    d = the distance traveled by the object

    v = the object's velocity, which is the distance an object travels in a certain amount of time; the rate of motion or speed

    t = the time to travel the desired distance

From an organizational performance perspective, the second law of organizational motion states:

If an unbalanced force acts on an organization, the organization will change its status quo in how it thinks, behaves, and reacts.

---

[183] Hodanbosi, C. (1996). *The first and second laws of motion.* Edited by Jonathan G. Fairman. Retrieved on August 4, 2016, from https://www.grc.nasa.gov/www/k-12/WindTunnel/Activities/first2nd_lawsf_motion.html

This second law of organizational motion indicates how an organization thinks, behaves, and reacts based upon an unbalanced net sum of forces. If the net sum of forces is negative, then the organization will dig its heels in and embed or embrace its status quo to an even greater degree. If the net sum of forces is zero, its status quo will not change. Neither a negative nor a zero net sum of forces is desired for a performance improvement focused endeavor nor to move an organization to a desired future state. A positive net sum of forces is desired; this force will create an increase in an organization's performance level or will move an organization toward the future state desired.

This second law of organizational motion has applicability on describing an object's motion. Using the first formula associated with the second law of organizational motion ($F_O = m_O a_O$), the greater the organizational mass the greater is the magnitude of force necessary to change it from its current state or to change its direction. Additionally, utilizing another formula of the second law of organizational motion ($d_O = v_O t_O$; namely $t_O = d_O/v_O$), the time required to move an organization from its current state to its future state is a function of the distance between its two states and how fast the organization is moving toward the desired future state.

The third law of motion states:

For every action, there is an equal and opposite reaction.[184]

From an organizational performance perspective, the third law of organizational motion is the same as the Newton's third law of motion. Therefore, this third law indicates there are always two actions or forces at work for every single interaction; there is an action and a reaction. These two actions or forces, though in opposite directions, are equal in strength if the body being acted upon by the forces does not move.

This law is the basis for understanding how airplanes fly. If the force, in this case the air pressure, pushing down on the body, which is the airplane's wing, is equal to the pressure pushing up against the wing the airplane stays level or on the ground. As soon as the air pressure pushing down on the wing is less than the pressure from below the wing exists, the airplane will rise or go up. Of course, the opposite is true to make the airplane drop or go down.

This law is also the basis for understanding organizational performance. So, if an action or force is applied to an organization and the organization does not move toward the desired future state, then the reaction the organization is exerting in the opposite direction is either equal to or greater than the applied force. Using the

---

[184] Hall, N. (2015). *The third law of motion*. Retrieved on August 4, 2016, from https://www.grc.nasa.gov/ www/k-12/airplane/newton3.html

second law of organizational motion, this result means the net sum of forces is zero or negative respectively. Once the net sum of forces is positive, the organization will begin to move toward the desired future state.

Zeroth Law of Thermodynamics (Thermal Equilibrium)

Thermodynamics is the branch of physical science dealing with the relationship between heat and other forms of energy and, by extension, of the relationships between all forms of energy. Energy is a system's ability to perform work.

The Zeroth Law of Thermodynamics presents to the property of temperature. It indicates two objects are considered to be in a state of thermal equilibrium when they are not passing heat or energy between each other even though they possess the ability to do so. Heat and energy flows from the high temperatures to the colder temperatures. Therefore, when two objects are in thermal equilibrium, the two objects are the same temperature.

One will experience this Law of thermodynamics when you jump into a cold swimming pool in the wintertime. Because of the thermal differential, meaning the pool's water is a lower temperature than the temperature of your body, heat and energy will flow from your body to the pool's water. The goal is your body attempting to warm up the pool water. Eventually, you start to shake which is the body's natural way to generate more heat and energy. Unfortunately, when thermal equilibrium occurs and your body is the same temperature as the cold winter pool water, your body's temperature is probably not warm enough to maintain life. A medical emergency occurs when your body loses heat faster than it can produce it, causing a dangerously low body temperature, a state called Hypothermia then sets in. Death may occur shortly thereafter. This state is probably not a desirable one for you.

From a perspective of organizational performance, if an organization is just existing in their environment and is not just changing, the organization may be in thermal equilibrium with its surrounding environment. This law correlates well with the first two laws of organizational motion as components of the theory of Newtonian Mechanics. The first law of organizational motion states a body's tendency is to maintain its status quo in how it thinks, behaves, and reacts unless a force, either internal or external, acts on it. The second law of organizational motion indicates if an unbalanced force acts on a body, the body will change its status quo in how it thinks, behaves, and reacts.

To change an organization's status quo heat and energy must be applied to it, whereas the heat and energy is greater than the existing organizational hear and energy level, so the heat and energy will flow from the high heat and energy source to the lower heat and energy level system. The organization will continue to change as long as the applied heat and energy is greater than its own. Once the organization achieves thermal equilibrium, the change effort will stabilize at this new level.

First Law of Thermodynamics

The First Law of Thermodynamics, also known as the Law of Energy Conservation, states every system has a property called, Energy, which utilizes the symbol, E, to denote it. All the energy within a closed system is the sum (Σ) of all of the various energies within it. Energy comes in many forms. To name a few, there is chemical energy, thermal energy, electric energy, and nuclear energy. The two main classes of energy, which are Internal (E_U) and External (E_X). External energy may be subdivided into kinetic energy (E_K) and potential energy (E_P), equating respectively to actuality (energy in motion) and potentiality (energy at rest).[185] All energy is measured using the unit Joule (J). As this is not a physics course, let us stop here by introducing these concepts.

To continue, the First Law of Thermodynamics, also known as the Law of Energy Conservation, purports energy cannot be created or destroyed in an isolated system; energy can only be transferred or changed from one form to another.[186] Therefore, this law of physics indicates the energy of a closed system will not change. For it to change, it must be an open system so external forces can influence or act on the system. An organization is an open system.

Open system theory, initially developed by Ludwig von Bertanlanffy in 1956 defined the concept of a system, where all systems contains components, which are interdependent upon each other. In physics, a closed system is permeable to energy but not to matter. An open system, by contrast, is one whose border is permeable to both energy and mass. A closed system contains only so much energy; it has a limited supply of energy. In contrast to a closed system, an open system has an infinite supply of energy, which cannot be depleted because there is always energy available from its surrounding environment.

As an example of the First Law of Thermodynamics, a water wheel whose river has run dry cannot turn. The potential energy it has is not enough to turn it and it cannot generate energy on its own. However, because this is an open system, if the river begins to run with water again, the running river water will turn the water wheel thus its potential energy is turning into kinetic energy. Because the wheel's axle is connected to an electrical generator, when the wheel turns the generator will

---

[185] Brenner, J. (2008). *Logic in reality* (illustrated ed.). New York, NJ: Springer Science & Business Media. p. 93.
[186] Boundless. (02 June 2016). *Boundless chemistry: The three laws of thermodynamics.* Retrieved February 13, 2017, from https://www.boundless.com/chemistry/textbooks/boundless-chemistry-textbook/thermodynamics-17/the-laws-of-thermodynamics-123/the-three-laws-of-thermodynamics-496-3601/

also turn. The turning generator will create electricity then the light bulb to which it is connected will light up when the switch is turned on. When the bulb lights up, it will create light and heat. One might think energy is created. However, this concept is false. Using the First Law of Thermodynamics, the energy from the running river water is transferred to light bulb via the spinning water wheel, generator, and wire.

This law indicates a change in heat (Q) or work (W) will change the system's internal differential of energy ΔE_U. This energy differential is also represented by $\Delta E_U = E_F - E_i$, whereas E_F is the system's final energy level and E_i is its initial energy level. The variables effecting the system's energy is heat and work. So, the First Law of Thermodynamics expressed as a formula is:

$$E_F - E_i = \Delta E_U$$

Or

$$\Delta E_U = Q - W$$

Another way of expressing the formula is the energy of the surrounding environment equals the amount of energy in the system plus the level of work. The corresponding formula is:

$$\Delta E_U + W = Q$$

Or

$$(E_F - E_i) + W = Q$$

Whereas:

ΔE_U = Change in internal energy in a system

Q = The heat energy absorbed or released by the system; note both heat and work energy is measured in Joules. Therefore, the heat energy is either added to or is taken away from the system. The heat energy transfer level is a positive number when the system absorbs the heat or when heat flows from the environment into the system. The heat energy transfer level is a negative number when the system releases heat or when the heat energy flows from the system out into the environment.

W = The work energy done by the system on the environment or the work energy done by the environment onto the system; note both heat and work energy is measured in Joules. The work energy level is a negative number when the surrounding environment does work on the system or the work energy transfer is from the environment into the system. The work energy level is a positive number when the system does work on its surrounding environment or the work energy flows from the system into the environment.

To assist in understanding this law, consider an engine does 3000 Joules of work energy onto its surrounding environment and releases 4000 Joules of heat energy into its surrounding environment. So, using the formula $\Delta E = Q - W$ and filling in the numbers then ΔE = − 4000 −3000 or −7000 Joules in the total change of internal energy. In addition, the negative number symbolizes the energy left the system.

If the same system absorbed 3000 Joules of heat energy from its surrounding environment while doing 4000 Joules of work energy on its surrounding environment, then working the formula now, ΔE is (+3000) Joules [Q; Heat energy coming in] − (+4000) Joules [W; Work energy going out]; therefore, ΔE = Q − W = −1000. The negative sign indicates the energy exited the system and went into the environment.

In the act of redefining this law to take on an organizational perspective, its name is converted to the *First Law of Organizational Thermodynamics*, also known as the *Law of Conservation of Organizational Energy*.

This organizational law indicates a change in organizational heat (Q_O) or work (W_O) will change the system's internal differential of energy ΔE_{OU}. This energy differential is also represented by $\Delta E_{OU} = E_{OF} − E_{Oi}$, whereas E_{OF} is the system's final energy level and E_{Oi} is its initial energy level. The variables effecting the system's energy is heat and work. So, the First Law of Thermodynamics expressed as a formula is:

$$E_{OF} - E_{Oi} = \Delta E_{OU}$$

Or

$$\Delta E_{OU} = Q_O - W_O$$

Another way of expressing the formula is the energy of the surrounding environment equals the amount of energy in the system plus the level of work. The corresponding formula is:

$$\Delta E_{OU} + W_O = Q_O$$

Or

$$(E_{OF} - E_{Oi}) + W_O = Q_O$$

Whereas:

ΔE_{OU} = Change in internal energy in an organizational system

Q_O = The heat energy absorbed or released by the organizational system; note both organizational heat and work energy is measured in Joules. Therefore, the organizational heat energy either is added to or is taken away from the organizational system. The organizational heat-energy transfer level is a positive number when the organizational system absorbs the heat or when heat flows from the environment into the organizational system. The organizational heat-energy transfer level is a negative number when the organizational system releases heat or when the organizational heat energy flows from the organizational system out into the environment.

W_O = The work energy done by the organizational system on the environment or the work energy done by the environment onto the organizational system; note both organizational heat and work energy is measured in Joules. The organizational work energy level is a negative number when the surrounding environment does work on the organizational system or the organizational work energy transfer is from the environment into the organizational system. The organizational work energy level is a positive number when the organizational system does work on its surrounding environment or the organizational work energy flows from the organizational system into the environment.

The application of the First Law of Organizational Thermodynamics is now in order. To begin, there are some operational definitions necessary to ensure common understanding. The organizational system has a permeable boundary, which depicts the open organizational system. Every item contained within the boundary is the organizational system whereas everything external to boundary is the surroundings or environment.

As mentioned, a closed system has a limited amount of internal energy; it cannot receive energy from other sources and cannot create more energy. Fortunately, an organization is an open system. The First Law of Organizational Thermodynamics indicates all organizational systems, because they are open, have energy sources. These energy sources come in the form of a wide variety of resources. To name just a few, there are internal human resources, financial resources, educational resources, and industry resources. These internal resources may also have counterparts described as external environment resources, such as customer resources, regulatory resources, banking resources, and economic resources. All of these resources and many more unmentioned ones are available to provide energy to the organizational system. The work equates to products, services, expertise, and support. Optimally, this work is created by and within the organizational system then is transferred to the surroundings or environment for a profit. If the work is kept within the system and not transferred to the environment, then the organization would be working in the red, at a loss, or considered to be working on overhead. However, if the work is created within the system and transferred to the environment, then the organization is working in the black and creating profits. The effective use of all of the internal and external resources as each provides energy to the organizational system dictate the success level of the organizational system as it strives toward high performance.

Second Law of Thermodynamics

The second law of thermodynamics states the entropy of any isolated, closed system always increases resulting in the death of the system.[187] Entropy, symbolized by S, is a measure of the unavailable energy in a closed thermodynamic system. From a broad perspective, entropy is the degree of disorder or uncertainty in a system.[188] The change in entropy is symbolized by ΔS. Entropy varies directly with any reversible change in heat in the system and inversely with the temperature of the system. In regards to the correlation between entropy and heat, these two points means entropy will adjust in an opposite fashion by the same proportion as the amount of heat is adjusted and if the temperature rises, then the entropy level goes down. For example, if heat goes up by 5 Joules or the temperature rises by 5 degrees Fahrenheit, entropy will go down by 5 Joules and 5 degrees. The formula for this action is:

$$\Delta S_U = \int \frac{\delta Q_{rev}}{T}$$

Whereas:

ΔS_U = Change in entropy in a system

δQ_{rev} = An incremental reversible transfer of heat into the system. If heat is transferred out, then the sign would be reversed giving a decrease in entropy of the system.

T = The system's temperature

An example of second law of thermodynamics is a car moves on its own power because the potential energy held by the fuel is converted to mechanical energy by the combustion engine. The car will stop running once the potential energy in the fuel is expended. As the car's fuel energy dwindles, the entropy level is going up. The vehicle's entropy level will reach its maximum level immediately once the car stops. The only way to lower the car's entropy level is to refuel the vehicle with more fuel with its potential energy. Within a closed system, the potential energy of an organization will always be less than its initial level if the system's energy level is not replenishing resulting in entropy levels going up.

Fortunately, an organization is an open system. Therefore, thinking from an organizational perspective and its open system, the second law of organizational

---

[187] Ibid

[188] Merriam-Webster (n.d.). *Entropy – Definition*. Retrieved on February 22, 2017, from https://www.merriam-webster.com/dictionary/entropy

thermodynamics states, an organization's entropy levels increases resulting in the death of the organization unless energy is received from a source to maintain the organization. As with the first law of organizational thermodynamics, these energy resources come in many forms. These resources provide energy to the organizational system and its created work levels dictates is the organization is thriving or dying.

The formula for the second law of organizational thermodynamics is:

$$\Delta S_{OU} = \int \frac{\delta Q_{rev}}{T_O}$$

Whereas:

ΔS_{OU} = Change in entropy in an organizational system

δQO_{rev} = An incremental reversible transfer of heat into the organizational system. If heat is transferred out, then the sign would be reversed giving a decrease in entropy of the system.

T_O = The organizational system's temperature

Another formula to help to understand the dynamics of the second law of organizational thermodynamics as it is associated with the organization's ability to achieve their vision and mission is:

$$W_O = \sum \frac{E_E - E_O}{S}$$

Whereas:

W_O = Organizational Work level of an organizational system equates to assessing the organization's successful achievement of its vision and mission. If the results are positive and greater than one, then the organization is operating in the black and earning a profit and achieving its vision and mission. If the results are negative or less than one, then the organization is operating in the red and losing profits as well as not achieving its vision and mission.

E_E = Environmental Energy being infused in or being absorbed out of the organizational system. If the energy is coming into the organizational system, then the Environmental Energy level is positive. If the energy is being absorbed by the environment from the organizational system, then the Environmental Energy level is negative.

E_O = Organizational Energy being created by the organization. If the energy is being consumed by the organizational system, then the Organizational Energy level is positive. If the energy is being pushed out into the environment from the organizational system, then the Organizational Energy level is negative.

S = The organizational entropy level and equates to the amount of resources necessary to keep the organization solvent or to operate.

The application of this organizational work level formula determines ultimately an organization's successful achievement of its vision and mission. The goal is to have keep the Environmental Energy level as high as possible compared with or above the entropy level. Additionally, the organizational system wants to create more Organizational Energy with its given resources so the organization is pushing its organizational energy out to its environment. Lastly, the organization would like to keep the entropy levels as low as possible. Some attributes affecting the entropy levels is the cost of doing business, which includes, but not limited to such issues associated with,

- The separation between where the leaders want to take the organization and where the employees are headed
- The lack of customer satisfaction
- The lack of workforce engagement
- The level of internal and external organizational strife

The effective use of all of the internal and external resources as each provides energy to the organizational system dictate the success level of the organizational system as it strives toward high performance.

Third Law of Thermodynamics

The third law of thermodynamics states the entropy of a system approaches a constant value as the temperature approaches absolute zero.[189] This particular law of thermodynamics indicates absolute zero is considered the lower limit for the temperature of any system and there is only a process to get real close to absolute zero but it can never by obtained.

The third law of organizational thermodynamics is not quite as applicable as the other two laws; however, though minute, there is an applicability. The third law of

---

[189] Ibid

organizational thermodynamics indicates though an organization is not able to achieve a temperature of absolute zero. As it degrades toward absolute zero, one might think the organizational entropy levels would be increasing to maximum level. However, just like any living organism, an organization approaching a temperature of absolute zero, is for all practical purposes dead. Therefore, as an organization is approaching absolute zero and death, the level of entropy is approaching absolute zero too. Once a living organism dies, there is no more entropy either. This organizational state is not desirable; avoid it as much as possible.

Law of the Conservation of Momentum

People, in general, utilizes the word, Momentum, in everyday life. A sports team has momentum if they are ahead going into the last quarter of the game. Political candidates running for an office are picking up momentum when they are closing the gap with the front-runner or when the front-runner is pulling away from the rest of the pack. In general, people are stating one entity or body is trending or moving toward one outcome, namely a successful one, while others are trending or moving in the other direction.

Conservation, in physics, refers to the concept of some attribute is unchanging; the conserved attribute is constant as a function of time. There are three constant attributes in physics: energy, general momentum, and angular momentum. These three attributes are considered constant just to ease their understanding. The Law of the Conservation of Momentum, which applies only to *isolated objects or systems*, purports:

> The momentum of an object will not change unless an external force is applied on it or in some fashion influences it.

The concept of momentum is associated with the formula for the second law of motion. Momentum is a body's mass in motion.[190] It is how much mass is in how much motion and in what direction (a vector). The generalized, without a direction (vector) component, formula for momentum is:

$$p = mv$$

Whereas:

- p = the object's momentum
- m = the object's mass; how much matter it contains
- v = the object's velocity, which is the distance an object travels in a certain amount of time; the rate of motion or speed

Momentum is also a function of force. Force is a function of mass and acceleration ($f = ma$). Velocity is a function of acceleration and time ($v = at$). Therefore, if the

---

[190] The Physics Classroom. (n.d.). *Momentum - The physics classroom*. Retrieved on August 5, 2016, from https:// www.physicsclassroom.com/Class/momentum/u4l1a.cfm

above equation is rewritten with some substitutions, with "at" for velocity and force for "ma," the formula evolves in the below fashion:

$$p = mv$$
$$p = m(at), \text{ which is the same as } p = (ma)t; \text{ therefore,}$$
$$p = ft = J \text{ or } \Delta p = f(\Delta t) = \Delta J$$

Whereas:

- p = the object's momentum
- Δp = the change in the object's momentum, or impulse (J)
- v = the object's velocity, which is the distance an object travels in a certain amount of time; the rate of motion or speed
- a = the acceleration the force causes; it is how an object's velocity changes over time
- t = the time to travel the desired distance
- Δt = the change in time to travel the desired distance
- m = the object's mass; how much matter it contains
- f = the forces acting on an object
- J = the object's impulse
- ΔJ = the change in the object's impulse

The concept of momentum is directly associated with Newton's Third Law of Motion, which states for every action there is an equal but opposite reaction, or:

$$F_{AB} = -F_{BA}$$

Whereas:

- F_{AB} = the net sum forces of object A acting on object B
- F_{BA} = the net sum forces of object B acting on object A with the negative sign indicating it is in the opposite direction of F_{AB}

These two forces act on each other as long as they are in contact with each other. Contact, therefore, there is a function of time. The length of time two objects remain in contact with each other is represented as t_{AB} and t_{BA}. Keep in mind, t_{AB} and t_{BA} is equal to each other as one object cannot leave its contact with another object at a different time. Therefore, t_{AB} equals t_{BA}.

Another aspect of momentum is the concept of impulse (J). Impulse (J) is the change of momentum (Δp) and the interplay of impulse and momentum is explained in the impulse-momentum theorem. Because of this theorem, there is a direct correlation between how forces act on a body as a function of time and the motion of the body. An understanding of impulse is important because forces in the real world are normally not constant. Forces do to the dynamics of people, both internal and external to a system, move from zero to some level as a function of time. Of course, the dynamics of people are dependent upon many forces. Therefore, if one wants to increase the momentum of an object, the impulse must be added to it by pushing on it with a certain force for a certain amount of time. As force with time is the amount of the impulse this is the exact amount by which the momentum will increase. Remember, because this movement is based upon laws of motion, there is a direction (vector) component existing.

In using the above formulas, the resulting formula for impulse is:

$$F_{AB} t_{AB} = -F_{BA} t_{BA}$$

Whereas:

F_{AB} and t_{AB} = the net sum forces and time of object A acting on object B

F_{BA} and t_{Ba} = the net sum forces and time of object B acting on object A with the negative sign associated with F_{BA} indicating the force is in the opposite direction of F_{AB}

Remembering, impulse is equal to the change of momentum, using Newton's Third Law of Motion the change in two object's momenta is equal but in opposite directions, so:

$$\Delta p = \Delta J$$
$$\text{Object } 1_{ma(t)} = -\text{Object } 2_{ma(t)}$$
$$\text{Object } 1_{f(\Delta t)} = -\text{Object } 2_{f(\Delta t)}$$

Or, with the Law of the Conservation of Momentum,

$$\text{Object } 1_{ma(\Delta t)} + \text{Object } 2_{ma(\Delta t)} = 0 \text{ and Object } 1_{f(\Delta t)} + \text{Object } 2_{f(\Delta t)} = 0$$

Whereas:

Δp = the change in the object's momentum, which is a function of force and time

ΔJ = the change in the object's impulse, which is a function of force and time

t = the time to travel the desired distance

Δt = the change in time to travel the desired distance

f = the forces acting on an object, which is a function of mass and acceleration

a = the acceleration the force causes; it is how an object's velocity changes over time

m = the object's mass; how much matter it contains

In keeping with the adjustments of other laws to reflect organizations, the definition for the Law of the Conservation of Organizational Momentum is:

The momentum of an organization will not change unless an external force is applied on it or in some fashion influences it.

The formula for the Law of the Conservation of Organizational Momentum is:

$$p_o = m_o v_o$$

Whereas:

p_o = the organization's momentum

m_o = the organization's mass; how much matter it contains

v_o = the organization's velocity, which is the distance an object travels in a certain amount of time; the rate of motion or speed

The momentum of an organization is a function of the forces acting upon it. Organizational force is a function of its mass and acceleration ($f_o = m_o a_o$). Organizational velocity is a function of its acceleration and time ($v_o = a_o t_o$). Therefore, if the above equation is rewritten with some substitutions, with "$a_o t_o$" for the organizational velocity and organizational force for "$m_o a_o$," the formula evolves in the below fashion:

$$p_o = m_o v_o$$

$p_o = m_o (a_o t_o)$, which is the same as $p_o = (m_o a_o) t_o$; therefore,

$$p_o = f_o t_o \text{ or } \Delta p_o = f_o (\Delta t_o) = J_o$$

Whereas:

p_o = the organization's momentum

Δp_o = the organization's change in momentum, or impulse (J)

v_o = the organization's velocity, which is the distance an object travels in a certain amount of time; the rate of motion or speed

a_o = the acceleration the force causes; it is how an organization's velocity changes over time

t_o = the time to travel the desired distance

Δt_o = the change in time to travel the desired distance

m_o = the organization's mass; how much matter it contains

f_o = the forces acting on an organization

J_o = the organization's impulse; which like work is a change in energy

The Law of the Conservation of Organizational Momentum has applicability with the second law of organizational motion. Though one may use the saying, the fast moving car has a lot of momentum, a sports team, which is a type of organization, is also said to have momentum when on the move or, also referring to a sports team is the saying that the momentum has swung to them. In regards to the momentum formula ($p_o = m_o v_o$) of an organization, its momentum, mass, and velocity correlates in a positive fashion. An increase in either an organization's mass or velocity will create a proportional increase in its momentum.

Additionally, using the first formula associated with the second law of organizational motion ($F_O = m_O a_O$), the greater the organizational mass the greater is the magnitude of force necessary to change it from its current state or to change its direction.

Lastly, utilizing another formula of the second law of organizational motion ($d_O = v_O t_O$; namely $t_O = d_O/v_O$), the time required to move an organization from its current state to its future state is a function of the distance between its two states and how fast the organization is moving toward the desired future state.

Law of Gravity

The concept of gravity is taught quite early on in one's life. This concept is illustrated often with Newton watching an apple falling from a tree and concluding there must be some unseen force causing the apple to fall down as opposed to flying up. The force of gravity (F_g) provides credence to the saying *what goes up must come down*. There is also the acceleration of gravity (G), which is the acceleration experienced when only the force of gravity is acting on an object. The acceleration of gravity close to the surface of the earth is 9.8 m/s². The official definition of the law of gravity is:

> A law indicating any two objects, having mass, attract each other with a force equal to a constant (constant of gravitation) multiplied by the product of the mass of each object and divided by the square of the distance between the objects.[191]

This definition is explained mathematically as:

$$F_g = G [(m_1 m_2)/r^2]$$

Whereas:

F_g = the force of gravity
G = the acceleration of gravity, the universal constant
m_1 = the mass of object one
m_2 = the mass of object two
r = the separation distance between the objects

For clarity, a critical component of Newton's Law of Gravity is the quantity of mass. Many people associate mass and weight as being the same but they are not. However, they are related. Mass is a measure of how much material is in an object. Weight is actually just the gravitational force exerted on a certain object with a given mass. For example, a person having a certain amount of mass has a certain level of gravitational force exerted on it from the earth. In this particular case, the

---

[191] Law of Gravitation (n.d.). Definition: Law of Gravitation. Retrieved on March 11, 2017, from http://www.dictionary.com/browse/law-of-gravitation

gravitational force is translated into a person's weight, given normally in pounds if a person is in the United States.

A conclusion drawn, from the force of gravity formula, is given two objects, each of a certain mass, m_1 and m_2 respectively, the resulting level of gravitational force exerted on the two objects is F_g. Therefore, if the mass of object 1 doubles while the mass of object 2 remains the same, then F_g must also double. If the mass of each object doubles, then F_g must increase by a fold of four (4).

Another aspect of the formula for the force of gravity is its relationship with the separation distance between the objects. The inverse square law proposed by Newton suggests the force of gravity acting between any two objects is inversely proportional to the square of the separation distance between the object's centers. In other words, changing the separation distance (r) results in a change in the force of gravity acting between the objects. Since the two quantities are inversely proportional, an increase in one quantity results in a decrease in the value of the other quantity. Therefore, an increase in the separation distance causes a decrease in the force of gravity and a decrease in the separation distance causes an increase in the force of gravity. As an example, from the force of gravity formula, given two objects, each of a certain mass, m_1 and m_2 respectively, the resulting level of gravitational force exerted on the two objects is F_g. However, if the separation distance between the two objects doubles, then the force of gravity will be a quarter (¼) its original level. If the separation distance between the two objects is cut in half, then the force of gravity will be four (4) times its original level.

Additionally, one can see the factor by which the force of gravity is changed is the square of the factor by which the separation distance is changed. Therefore, if the separation distance is doubled (increased by a factor of 2), then the force of gravity is decreased by a factor of four (2 raised to the second power). Continuing the thought, if the separation distance (r) is tripled (increased by a factor of 3), then the force of gravity is decreased by a factor of nine (3 raised to the second power). If the mass of each object doubles but the separation distance also doubles, then F_g will remain the same as its original level.

The organizational law of gravitation is:

> A law indicating entities, which can be organizations or people, having mass, attracts each other with a force equal to a constant (constant of gravitation) multiplied by the product of the mass of each object and divided by the square of the distance between the objects.

William Reilly evolved this law to customers.[192] He stated customers would travel to larger retail companies because of the retail company's higher attraction. This higher attraction may be truly real or imaginary but to the customers it is real. The distance willing to be covered is proportional to the level of attraction for the retail company to meet the customer's need requiring fulfilled. In this particular case, the ability to fill a need and the customer's need is analogous of each entity's mass.

Conclusion

According to a 2013 worldwide, 142-country, research study conducted by the Gallup organization, only 13% of employees are engaged within the work environment.[193] An engaged employee is one who is committed to performing their jobs to the utmost of their abilities. According to the same study, 63% of the studies countries have employees, which are not engaged. These type of employees are not motivated, do not feel any obligation to their organizations, and do not see how their efforts play into contributing to the organization's goals. Lastly, the Gallup organization concluded 24% of the researched country's workforces are actively disengaged. This disengagement is synonymous with employees being unhappy and unproductive. This feeling and lack of action can spread like a cancer to these peoples' coworkers. In the United States and Canada, only 29% of their workers are engaged in their work, meaning they are passionately involved in it. Fifty-four percent are not engaged (essentially, sleepwalking through their work) and 18% are actively disengaged, meaning they act out their unhappiness on the job. Organizational leaders, to ensure the successful achievement of their organizations' strategic vision, mission, and goals, must implement some interventions to turn the non-engaged and the actively disengaged employees around. The development of these interventions begins with understanding their organizations.

Like the Maltese Falcon analogy, the more theories one uses to explain a point of study, the more likely that some level of the truth, some level of understanding will emerge. The closer one gets to the truth the better their school of thought is in predicting how future issues will evolve. Therefore, a multi-perspective psychological, biological, and physical approach through which to understand and explain people within the context of an organizational work environment provides the most holistic view of organizations and permits the widest understanding of how human beings work. A multi-perspective view through which to drive an organization toward high performance is the most valid.

---

[192] Reilly, W. (1931). *The law of retail gravitation*. New York, NY: Knickerbocker Press.
[193] Crabtree, S. (2013). *Worldwide, 13% of employees are engaged at work*. Retrieved on May 2, 2017, from http://www.gallup.com/poll/165269/worldwide-employees-engaged-work.aspx

This page left blank intentionally.

Chapter 6:
The Organizational Action Research Schemata

Introduction

Organizational leadership and management can be a challenge at best. The work environment, consisting of the integration of people and machines, must work seamlessly together for the highest level of efficiency. The organization may look, superficially, as if it is highly performing; however, in actuality, if the organization is not high performing, it may not correct itself on its own. Leaders first must be aware an issue or situation exists inhibiting the organization's performance. To obtain this awareness, there is a need to explore the inner work environment of organizations. After awareness exists, leaders can then make some type of decision to correct the issue or situation. Once the decision is implemented, a feedback mechanism is required to ensure the correction was effective or if another correction is needed. Riordan purported Action Research is a methodology exploring the reality of a social environment integrating science and the practitioner mentality of objectivity.[194] In general, this is Action Research.

Based upon a literature review, Action Research deals with nine general components. [195] [196] [197] [198] [199] [200] [201] [202]

To begin:

1. **Action-Focused**. It is research generating action rather than exploratory research about an action.

2. **Interactive**. Researchers conduct the research in conjunction with the organizational leaders and employees making it an interactive endeavor. While the endeavor is ongoing, there is a continuous feedback focus so it is dynamic and adapting.

---

[194] Riordan, P. (1995). The philosophy of action science. *Journal of Managerial Psychology*, 10 (6), 6-13.
[195] Foster, M. (1972). An introduction to the theory and practice of action research in work organizations. *Human Relations*, 25 (6), 529-556.
[196] Susman, G., & Evered, R. (1978). An assessment of the scientific merits of action research. *Administrative Science Quarterly*, 23 (4), 582-603.
[197] Peters, M., & Robinson, V. (1984). The origins and status of action research. *Journal of Applied Behavioral Science*, 20 (2), 113-124.
[198] Argyris, C., Putnam, R., & Smith, D. (1985). *Action science: Concepts, methods, and skills for research and intervention*. San Francisco, CA: Jossey-Bass.
[199] Whyte, W. (1991). *Participatory Action Research*. Thousand Oaks, CA: Sage.
[200] Aguinis, H. (1993). Action research and scientific method: Presumed discrepancies and actual similarities. *Journal of Applied Behavioral Science*, 29 (4), 416-431.
[201] Greenwood, D., & Levin, M. (1998). *Introduction to action research*. Thousand Oaks, CA: Sage.
[202] Gummesson, E. (2000). *Qualitative methods in management* research (2nd ed.). Thousand Oaks, CA: Sage.

3. **Change-Focused**. Action Research is ultimately attempting change. The purpose is about creating and implementing solutions to issues and situations through a scientific approach. It also incorporates this scientific approach with those individuals, called stakeholders, who have a stake in correcting the issues and situations.[203] [204] [205]

4. **Informative**. It is valid research building upon the body of knowledge by potentially permitting generalizations to be made concerning the population of which the stakeholders, the sample, are a part.

5. **Methodical**. Action Research takes on a systematic process as it explores the issues and situations. This process begins with the engagement with the senior leadership to understand their thoughts on the organizational issues, situations, or symptoms inhibiting the company's performance.

6. **Holistic**. Action Research takes on a holistic perspective when studying the organizational system. The researcher is then able to drill down more effectively into the organization's subsystems by understanding how each section fits into the big organizational picture.[206]

7. **Ethical**. With all valid and reliable research, ethics is involved.[207] Security of data and treating the clients authentically are two points but they do not create a mutually inclusive list.

8. **Eclectic**. Action Research utilizes data from both qualitative and quantitative assessments. Additionally, because of the systems theory, it is acknowledged that the assessments can be, in of themselves, interventions and can thus be considered sources affecting change.

9. **Real-time**. The here-and-now is the primary timeframe in which Action Research is mostly focused. However, there may be a time whereas a retrospective process would be adequate. This type of research study would utilize reflection to promote organizational change.

---

[203] Beckhard, R., & Harris, R. (1987). *Organizational transitions: Managing complex change* (2nd ed.). Reading, MA: Addison-Wesley.

[204] Nadler, D., (1998). *Champions of change*. San Francisco, CA: Jossey-Bass.

[205] Coghlan, D., & Brannick, T., (2001). *Doing action research in your own organization*. London, UK: Sage.

[206] Nadler, D., & Tushman, M. (1984). A congruence model for diagnosing organizational behavior. In D. A. Kolb, I. M. Rubin, and J. M. McIntyre (eds), *Organizational Psychology, Readings on Human Behavior in Organizations* (4th ed.), Englewood Cliffs, NJ: Prentice-Hall. pp. 587-603.

[207] Coghlan, D., & Brannick, T., (2001). *Doing action research in your own organization*. London, UK: Sage.

Action Research is normally considered as beginning in America with the onset of Kurt Levin's research as a social scientist. It began from an individualist perspective with the focus being how one can improve themselves. Self-improvement takes an introspective paradigm.[208] By looking inward while taking an aim at where or what one wants to go or do, one explores how they can change to better, or more efficiently, achieve their desires. Of course, as no one is an island and, from a systemic paradigm, a minute change somewhere in the system changes the whole system, there is a social implication or ramification to this initial form of action research. If one person changes for the better then the whole system, the social environment in which that person belongs, changes for the better too. A social environment is a community of interaction. A type of community is an organization of employment. An organization in which one works is a work environment and subsequently a social environment. Therefore, with all of this said, it is quite logical to have the original individualistic view of Action Research evolve to an organizational angle. This evolutionary transformation is called the Organizational Action Research Schemata (OARS).

Organizational Action Research Schemata is an introspective and interactive exploration of an organization to determine the work environment using a scientific methodology. More specifically, OAR explores those attributes potentially inhibiting the organization from achieving its goals and objectives. OAR views firms both broadly, to understand the organizational context, but also microscopically, to gather the facts at the organizational DNA level. The organizational domain can be in the commercial, governmental, or not-for-profit environment. Any organization type can take advantage of Organizational Action Research. As the name, Organizational Action Research, emphatically states, it takes research-generated knowledge to affect action in the form of organizational change to improve the whole work environment.[209] From an abstract or strategic point of view, Organizational Action Research is a methodology providing insight into the inner workings of organization as well as potentially developing new theories or furthering the baseline knowledge in a focus area.[210] This insight is generated from a holistic, 360-degree view of the organization.[211] Additionally, this insight assists the organizational leadership in their decision making process to develop

---

[208] Elliott, J. (1991). *Action research for educational change*. Buckingham, England: Open University Press.
[209] Dick, B. (2002). What is action research? Retreived on September 19, 2010, from http://www.scu.edu.au/schools/gcm/ar/whatisar.html
[210] Elden, M., & Chisholm, R. (1993). Emerging varieties of action research: Introduction to the special issue. *Human Relations*, 46 (2), 121-142.
[211] Nadler, D., & Tushman, M. (1984). A congruence model for diagnosing organizational behavior. In D. A. Kolb, I. M. Rubin, and J. M. McIntyre (eds), *Organizational Psychology, Readings on Human Behavior in Organizations* (4th ed.), Englewood Cliffs, NJ: Prentice-Hall. pp. 587-603.

interventions for the issues and situations they face prohibiting the organization's performance.

This perspective, on OARS, indicates it is truly a scientific-practitioner endeavor. As such, it focuses on solving an issue or situation using a scientific regiment of ethics, integrity, validity, and reliability. Solving issues and situations is fundamentally about organizational change. Additionally, there is a desire to contribute to the body of knowledge on the issue or situation.[212] A scientific-practitioner endeavor follows common research practices. It begins with an investigation embedded in theoretical orientation. This activity is followed by empirical, objective testing coupled with data analysis. Lastly, there is reflection, conclusions drawn based upon the outcomes followed by documentation of the research.

To expand upon these research practices, investigation entails meeting with the organizational leadership to join with them in exploring, from their perspective, what if any are the issues and situations residing within the organization. Joining is the process of creating an authentic, open, honest relationship with whom the researcher interacts. Also, paramount to joining with the organization is, once issues or situations seem to exist, ensuring the leader understands change is necessary and can be achieved, a desired end state is articulated and agreed upon, and agree to work with researcher to both develop and implement the intervention plan.[213] [214] [215] Other investigative actions include qualitative research with the organizational masses to obtain their perspective on the potential issues and situations. Additionally, a literature review on the issues and situations along with any past research and possible obtaining other experts view, if necessary, would be prudent. Having a theoretical grounding permits thoughts on potential reasons to explain the issues and situations. Subsequently, the theoretical assists in the creation of research questions and interventional hypotheses to test. Next, empirical, objective testing, data collection occurs. Data collection can be through the traditional methods of qualitative and quantitative tools. Like all valid research, the use of these tools requires forethought on how best these tools are injected into the organizational work environment. One must remember, from a systemic perspective, just the injection of these tools can affect change. Lastly, as with all research, data analysis, reflection to draw conclusions, and documentation followed

---

[212] Reason, P. (1999). Integrating action and reflection through co-operative inquiry. *Management Learning*, 30 (2), 207-226.
[213] Beckhard, R., & Harris, R. (1987). *Organizational transitions: Managing complex change* (2nd ed.). Reading, MA: Addison-Wesley.
[214] Nadler, D., (1998). *Champions of change*. San Francisco, CA: Jossey-Bass.
[215] Coghlan, D., & Brannick, T., (2001). *Doing action research in your own organization*. London, UK: Sage.

by the possibility of future research winds down the activity. As the data analysis is the foundation upon which reflection and conclusions are based, the statistics utilized must be sound. With the base solid, the documentation capturing the whole research but, more importantly, the results will be ethical, valid, and reliable. This activity is the background for a scientific-practitioner endeavor.

The scientific-practitioner is an Industrial/Organizational Psychologist, also known as the researcher. The researcher takes on two personas or portrays two models.[216] One model is as an expert. This expert model is much like a medical patient going to a doctor; hence, it is also known as the doctor-patient model. In this situation, the client contacts the I/O Psychologist, the researcher, to discuss their organization's issues, situations, or symptoms inhibiting performance. The client wants relief from these presented items. The researcher listens, conducts their own assessment, formulates an intervention, injects the intervention into the organizational system, re-assesses the organization, and adjusts the intervention as necessary. As one can see, in general, it mirrors the activity within a doctor's office. The second model is the consultant model. With the injection of the intervention into the organizational system, the client needs assistance with implementing the intervention. This assistance comes in the form of an I/O Psychologist working as a consultant or facilitator.[217] [218] [219] In this model, the I/O Psychologist with the client develops and implements enablers to increase the propensity that the intervention will achieve its desired end state. One such enabler would be a communication plan to build ownership and buy-in by the organizational membership to the intervention.

As mentioned, as a scientific-practitioner endeavor, OAR follows common research practices. Like all valid research, it has a particular methodology by which it is conducted. This methodology is well grounded by being similar, by nature, to other research practices. Carr and Kemmis purported the steps for Action Research, in general, to being reconnaissance, planning, implementation, observation, and reflection.[220] OAR takes on similar steps; however, the steps are called schema. There is not a tremendous difference between the previously mentioned steps and OARS' schema; however, the schema is the result of dissecting the steps. This dissection leads to the removal or separation of multiple but distinct activities being conducted within each step. The Organizational Action Research Schemata schema

---

[216] Schein, E. (1999). *Process consultation revisited: Building the helping relationship.* Reading, MA: Addison-Wesley.
[217] Schein, E. (1987). *The clinical perspective in fieldwork.* Thousand Oaks, CA: Sage.
[218] Schein, E. (1995). Process consultation, action research, and clinical inquiry: Are they the same? *Journal of Managerial Psychology*, 10 (6), 14-19.
[219] Coghlan, D. (1994). Research as a process of change: Action science in organizations. *Irish Business and Administrative Research*, 11 (1), 119-121.
[220] Carr, W., & Kemmis, S. (1986). *Becoming critical.* Lewes, England: Falmer Press.

are engagement, diagnosis, planning, implementation, reflection, and disengagement. Collectively, the Organizational Action Research Schemata provides a path leading ultimately to organizational high performance.

The Schemata

Schema 1: Engagement

As Organizational Action Research is both a valid and reliable process through which an organization's issues, situations, and symptoms affecting its performance in a negative fashion can be overcome. Not everyone has the knowledge, skills, and abilities (KSAs) to conduct an OAR study. One person who does have the KSAs is an Industrial / Organizational Psychologist. However, even with having the KSAs, a scientific-practitioner should want to share what they know to improve upon the breadth and width of the body of knowledge dealing with OAR. Up to this point, unfortunately, there seems not to be much of an effort to expand on the methodology of conducting OAR. This lack of living up to what is seen as a responsibility to share is the motivation for presenting not only this book but also the methodology for OAR, which begins with Schema 1, Engagement. This schema is comprised of scripts purporting various activities related to beginning an OAR relationship with the organization's leadership to improve upon those performance inhibiting issues, situations, or symptoms.[221]

Schema 2: Diagnosis

Once the Engagement schema is over with the conclusion of the Contracting act, the Organizational Action Research commences more formally with the Schema 2: Diagnosis. The Schema 2: Diagnosis initiates the exploration of the organization's current work environment. This Schema 2: Diagnosis is about inquiry. The researcher engages with the client to diagnose and eventually treat the organization's dysfunctions and pathologies.[222] [223] The client, like a patient, may disclose multiple presenting issues or situations. Maintaining the medical analogy, these are the organization's symptoms. These symptoms are acknowledged and validated as to possibly existing in the organizational work environment; however, like a doctor, the researcher is obligated to independently and objectively confirming these symptoms as well as determining if there are any other symptoms to why the organization is how it is. Both a broad and in-depth exploration of the organization will bring about a valid diagnosis. By having an accurate and reliable

---

[221] Hult, M. and Lennung, S. (1980). Towards a definition of action research: A note and a bibliography. *Journal of Management Studies*, 17 (2), 241-250.

[222] Schein, E.H. (1997). Organizational learning: What is new? In R.A. Rahim, R.T. Golembiewski, & L.E. Pate (eds), *Current Topics in Management*. Greenwich, CT: JAI Press. (Vol. 2, pp. 14-26).

[223] Schein, E. (2001). Clinical inquiry/research. In P. Reason & H. Bradbury (eds). *Handbook of Action Research*. London: Sage. (pp. 228-237).

diagnosis, thus a valid diagnosis, both the researcher and the client has a common operating picture of the organization's work environment.[224] This diagnosis drives Schema 3: Planning.

Schema 3: Planning

The purpose of data analysis is to be the impetus for activity. In this case, the information gleaned from the analysis feeds the Schema 3: Planning. Similar to the data analysis process, the Schema 3: Planning is performed or conducted collaboratively with the client.[225] This activity is the catalyst for permitting the client to claim and accept the issue or situation as theirs for which they should be part of the Planning stage. The overall goal of the Schema 3: Planning is working through a solution making process.

Planning is the art of decision making through an established systematic process. It is a sequential, exhaustive, intentional process, which, at times, can be time consuming. It is an adaptation of the Military Decision Making Process (MDMP) taught to every Officer, commissioned and noncommissioned, in the U.S. Army. Planning assists the researcher and the client to develop an intervention plan designed to change the organization in such a way to achieve a desired end state. The decision on a particular plan is developed by utilizing such attributes as diligence, sound reasoning as well as organizational and professional knowledge. It is a process of analytically and objectively comparing and contrasting various interventions in the attempt to decide upon the intervention having the greatest propensity of resulting in the desired organizational end state. This planning drives Schema 4: Implementation.

Schema 4: Implementation

As has been presented throughout the OAR, the Schema 4: Implementation is a dual and integrated effort between, one, the client and the researcher as well as, two, the researcher and the scholarly community.[226] [227] Though there could be an argument made stating both relationships mentioned are equally important, it is contended the first relationship between the client and the researcher is most important. Once more using the medical model, the client represents the patient. They are a paying client. Therefore, they are the most important member of any relationship with the researcher.

---

[224] Cunningham, J. (1993). *Action research and organizational development*. Westport, CT: Praeger.

[225] Beckhard, R., & Harris, R. (1987). *Organizational transitions: Managing complex change* (2nd ed.). Reading, MA: Addison-Wesley.

[226] Kemmis, S., & McTaggart, R. (1988). *The action research planner*. Victoria, AU: Deakin University.

[227] McKay, J., & Marshall, P. (2001). The dual imperatives of action research. *Information Technology and People*, 14 (1), 46–59.

To create the propensity of successfully obtaining the desired end state that the intervention is designed to achieve, both the client and the researcher must at least be equally motivated to affect positive change in the organizational work environment. If there is an imbalance in motivation, the likelihood of achieving the desired end state lessens. Once the client and the researcher are in agreement as to the most effective intervention for the diagnosed organizational issues or situations, the client implements the intervention through guidance with the researcher. Client implementation assists in creating client ownership of the issues or situations as well as buy-in into the intervention, the solution to their issues or situations. This implementation drives Schema 5: Reflection.

Schema 5: Reflection

Reflection is a cognitive process by which one can learn about a subject of interest. It is experiential learning grounded in the social environment upon which it is based.[228][229] The military calls it an After Action Review. Schema 5: Reflection is a purposeful, thoughtful activity designed to consider what the desired goal was, what was achieved, what was done well, and what can be improved upon. In OAR, the scientific-practitioner and the organizational client leadership are active participants in this process.[230] The information gleaned from monitoring, journaling, and post-evaluation research provides the necessary feedback to determine the effectiveness of the OARS process. It is necessary to know if the intervention changed the organization to reflect the desired end state or goal. If it did, all is well. However, if it did not, then the spiral process is repeated. This reflection drives Schema 6: Disengagement.

Schema 6: Disengagement

The ending of an OAR endeavor is as important as initiating it. The strength of OAR is its methodology. It takes on the characteristics of any ethical and valid research study; every aspect of OAR is set and repeatable. All the activity of OAR is transparent. There is no hidden process. The Schema 6: Disengagement mirrors this methodology. This disengagement drives Schema 7: Epilogue.

Schema 7: Epilogue

This Schema 7: Epilogue is somewhat a reflective activity. It is the final activity of the specific OAR endeavor. It is the time the Industrial/Organizational Psychologist, aka the researcher, sits down and performs two activities. First, they assimilate all that occurred during the client engagement and, second, puts pen to paper or fingertips to keyboard so to attempt to generalize the activity and

---

[228] Dewey, J. (1933). *How we think*. New York, NY: D. C. Heath.
[229] Vygotsky, L. (1962). *Thought and language*. (E.H. G. Vakar, Trans.). Cambridge, MA: MIT Press.
[230] Schön, D. (1983). *The reflective practitioner*. New York, NY: Basic Books.

subsequently, generate a theory to feed the existing body of knowledge on the subject.

Conclusion

People want to be part of a high performing organization. They want to be part of a team in which the operational definition is a group of persons, described as being on the cutting edge or being where the rubber meets the road. They want to work together in a structured environment, which effectively blends their needs with the organizational needs. They want to achieve, in a meaningful fashion, a goal that is bigger, larger, and more robust than they are and is contributory in a great way to society and, subsequently, considered as having a meaningful purpose. This statement is the operational definition of a high performing organization.

Individually, people bring their collective blueprint to the organization. An individual's blueprint is comprised of all that created the person to be who they are. It is their education level, their collective ancestral past, their biological makeup, and their social, cognitive, behavioral, affective influences, both internal and external. An individual blueprint is a blending of all of their past and present attributes defining them. The integration of all the attributes comprising of the individual blueprints as well as how well they function from an interrelationship standpoint creates the organizational blueprint.

The Organizational Action Research Schemata, as a foundational component of organizational high performance, incorporates studying organizational blueprints. The study of the organization's blueprint provides insight into their maladaptive issues or situations. The data is associated with understanding all information comprising of the organizational diversity makeup. This insight is illuminated with data related to such constructs as organizational characteristics, patterns, knowledge, skills, and values.

Understanding these organizational constructs is accomplished through the study of the individuals comprising the organization. Organizations, groups, sections, and teams comprise of individuals. Though from a Gestalt perspective, these entities may demonstrate a greater phenomenon than the sum of their parts, namely their membership, the individual people, the study of these individuals is necessary to extrapolate the information about the whole entity. From a systemic viewpoint, the organization is a function of its individualistic parts. The phenomenon, when working at an optimum performance level, creates a greater product or service in a more efficient way. This organizational phenomenon could be described as an organizational person.

Just like people, organizations from one company to another are different though, also like people, they all have commonalities. As an example, organizations have Chief Executive Officers, Chief Operations Officers, Supervisors, and

Secretaries; however, the comprising organizational constructs, as mentioned, are different. All people have bodies, brains, hearts, stomachs, and lungs but, between individuals, how each of these parts interacts with each other may be different or less efficient. By understanding the complexity of the individual parts and their blueprints, the organizational phenomenon, the organizational blueprint, begins to be understood.

In conclusion, with understanding, the issue or situation inhibiting the organization's performance can be overcome. The Organizational Action Research Schemata is the methodology assisting an organization toward high performance.

Chapter 7: Epilogue

Introduction

A high-performance workplace is an organizational state of mind whereas the people that comprise the organization are happy, fully of pep and energy, and working in a fun filled as well as an enthusiastic and optimistic environment.[231] This type of workplace epitomizes an organization that works together toward a common objective via a particular strategy accepted by all. Everyone, executives, managers, supervisors, and workers, are driven toward a common end state. The U.S. Department of Labor, Office of American Workplace (OAW) in a publication called *Road to High-Performance Workplaces: A Guide to Better Jobs and Better Business Results* prescribed four characteristics for which high performance workplaces should strive.[232] These characteristics were labeled "(a) skills and information; (b) participation, organization, and partnership; (c) compensation, security, and the work environment; and (d) putting it all together (5-6)." As one can easily note, the growing standard is to strive toward a high-performance workplace.[233]

Fundamentals of Organizational High Performance

The fundamentals of organizational high performance are comprised of the concepts held within the overarching below five areas. As Steve Covey said in his book, the *Seven Habits of Highly Successful People*, seek first to understand. Therefore, for an organization to achieve high performance, its leaders and employees must first understand the concepts underlying within the five areas then, most importantly, its leaders and employees must apply these concepts. Without implementation, no results can be realized.

The Management System

A Gestalt end state is the objective of the Management System. The organization utilizing the prescribed Management System will achieve more than the sum of each of its parts. An organization attempting to maximize their operational performance is enabling its workforce to take advantage of all

---

[231] Welbourne, T. (n.d.). High performance workplace and high performance leaders: February leadership pulse. HR.com. Retrieved on November, 27, 2005 from http://www.eepulse.com/documents/pdfs/high-perf-wkplace-030804.pdf.

[232] Japan Institute of Labour (2003). Developing the measures and checklists for the diagnosis and motivation of workplace. Japan Institute of Labour Publication, 161, 1-19. Retrieved on November 27, 2005 from http://www.jil.go.jp/english/ documents/JILNo161.pdf.

[233] Walsworth, S. (2005). Globalization, high performance workplace practices and unions: Recent evidence from the Canadian workplace and employee survey. Retrieved on November 27, 2005, from http://cerf.mcmaster.ca/conferences/workplace05/Walsworth.pdf.

organizational resources, that being people, processes, technology, and financials. The ultimate end state is increased functionality as well as performance. Optimal stakeholder and customer service is accomplished at low-cost with a high-variety of products, services, and expertise. The organization's processes and technology as well as its effective and efficient use of financials enable operations to achieve this low-cost, high-variety customer-focus paradigm. The end state is an organization moving toward high performance.

The Business Model

The Business Model delineates the required attributes an organization must consider and have so to become high performing. The heart of a high performance organization is its core values and goals. An organization not knowing what they stand for or where they are going will not easily, or not at all, achieve high performance. The overarching external influence of the organization's environment influences much in regards to how the rest of the business model components are developed and subsequently delivers results complementing the organization with its external environment.

Organizational leaders must have an understanding of just what is a high performance organization. The holistic business model, presented in Figure 3, provides the organizational components in which to focus on when an organization is moving toward high performance. All organizations have these components; however, their quality and level is what determines the difference between mediocre or high performance organizations.

The Leadership Standard

The quality of the leadership or management has a direct correlation to the productivity or performance of the organization.[234] The financial rewards of the organization are the measure by which one could evaluate the performance of an organization's leadership and management personnel.[235][236] Department of the Army defines leadership as the act of "influencing people -- by providing purpose, direction, and motivation -- while operating to accomplish the mission and improving the organization (p. 4)."[237] One should recognize these qualities of

---

[234] Flynn, B., Schroeder, R., & Sakabibara, S. (1995). The impact of quality management practices on performance and competitive advantage. *Decision Sciences*, 26(5), 659-691.

[235] Boyatzis, R. (1999). The financial impact of competencies in leadership and management of consulting firms. *Department of Organizational Behavior Working Paper*, Case Western Reserve University, Cleveland.

[236] Goleman, D. (2000). Leadership that gets results. *Harvard Business Review*. Retrieved on October 25, 2008, from http://harvardbusiness.org/hb-main/resources/pdfs/comm/microsoft/leadership-that-gets-results.pdf

[237] Department of the Army (1999). *Field manual 22-100: Army leadership -- Be, know, do*. Washington, DC: Department of the Army.

providing purpose, direction, and motivation will dramatically influence employees to achieve organizational objectives. The importance of leadership and its impact on performance has been well noted. Maddux and Wingfield pointed out leadership is team building.[238] If the organization is a team, the business will work as one to accomplish its goals. From a Gestalt perspective, the end state accomplished will be greater than the individual sum of the parts.[239] From this Gestalt perspective, the organization will then achieve high performance.

The Organizational Science

The Organizational Science presents the universal theories and laws of psychology, biology, and physics through which to explain how the organization foundationally operates. Through this understanding, the theories and laws can be utilized to create a valid plan designed to increase or enhance the organization's performance. Because the science of psychology and physics applies to all bodies, the theories and laws of organizational performance are considered universal because they apply to all organizational bodies and are thus industry nonspecific. The goal of these generalized and synthesized explanations is to provide a synopsis of each theory and law as well as why and how it is applicable to organizations striving for high performance.

The Organizational Action Research Schemata

With every journey, it is required to know two points. The first is where one is at and the second is where one wants to go. With these two points known, one can chart a path from one to the other. The Organizational Action Research Schemata is a valid methodology through which to understand one's organization's current, as-is, state as well as its desired future, to-be, state. Additionally, with its holistic application, the process of how an organization can get from one state to the other can be determined as well as developing metrics so to know where the organization is during the journey and when the organization has arrived. In this particular case, the future, to-be, state is organizational high performance.

---

[238] Maddux, B., & Wingfield, B. (2003). *Team building: An exercise in leadership* (4th ed.). Menlo Park, CA: Crisp.

[239] Doren, D., McCutcheon, A., Evans, M., MacMillan, K., Hall, L., Pringle, D., et al. (September, 2004). Impact of the manager's span of control on leadership and performance. *Canadian Health Services Research Foundation Publication*. Retrieved on April 27, 2008, from http://www.chsrf.ca/final_research/ogc/pdf/ doren2_final.pdf

Conclusion

Organizations are an integrated conglomerate of relationships.[240] There are many types of relationships in just as many circumstances. Intertwined with relationships is the attachment theory. The attachment theory was the joint work of John Bowlby and Mary Ainsworth.[241] Drawing on concepts from ethnology, information processing, developmental psychology, and psychoanalysis, they formulated the basic tenets of the theory. The attachment theory has a definite application to a wide variety of situations where people are considered. Therefore, psychologists can use it in the exploration for understanding relationships within and between organizations.

Welsch and LaVan pointed out behaviorism, but more importantly the attachment theory, is paramount in studying organizational allegiance.[242] Such behavioral concepts of stimulus and reinforcement facilitate a level of attachment creating such a strong commitment the employee considers the work environment as pleasurable, desirable, and rewarding. Molnar and Rogers purported a philosophy called organization-environment relations and a subset of a systems resource approach.[243] Leaders desire to keep employees, who are productive and happy. To create such an employee, the leaders want to recognize those creating the desired work environment and organizational strategies must be developed.

Quite often leaders examining organizational effectiveness explore equipment or technological advances. It is accepted employees are interactive within the organization to which they belong.[244] It has not been determined as to why managers seem to ignore this valuable asset as an influencing factor in an organization's effectiveness or performance. Andrew Ure implored executives to consider the human factor, a third element of manufacturing behind the other two components, mechanical and commercial.[245] The human element of an

---

[240] Wittmann, W., & Hattrup, K. (2004). The relationship between performance in dynamic systems and intelligence. *Systems Research and Behavioral Science*, 21(4), 393–409.

[241] Ainsworth, M., & Bowlby, J. (1991). An Ethological Approach to Personality Development. *American Psychologist*, 46(4), 333-341.

[242] Welsch, H., & LaVan, H. (1981). Inter-relationships between organizational commitment and job characteristics, job satisfaction, professional behavior, and organizational climate. *Human Relations*, 34(12), 1079.

[243] Molnar, J., & Rogers, D. (1976). Organizational effectiveness: An empirical comparison of the goal and system resource approaches. *The Sociological Quarterly*, 17(3), 401-413.

[244] Newstrom, J., & Davis, K. (1993). *Organizational behavior: Human behavior at work*. New York, NY: McGraw-Hill.

[245] Ure, A. (1835). The Philosophy of Manufactures, 5-7, 23, 301. In J. F. C. Harrison (ed.), *Society and Politics in England, 1780-1960*, New York, NY: Harper & Row, 1965, pp. 144-46.

organization, with their knowledge and experience, may very well be a critical element of any organization.[246]

High performance people enable the creation of high performance organizations, whereas the entities are more responsive in these modern, ever-changing, competitive environments. The members of high performance organizations develop such characteristics as a shared vision, increased levels of trust and openness within the organization and team, as well as continuously learn through quality leadership. Because of these and all of the other attributes of high performance organizations, results are achieved that are far greater than the sum of the individual efforts.

Organizational high performance workplace is an organizational state of mind whereas the people comprising the organization are happy, full of pep and energy, and working in a fun filled as well as an enthusiastic and an optimistic environment.[247] This type of workplace epitomizes an organization working together toward a common objective via a particular strategy accepted by all whereas everyone is driven toward a common end state. The U.S. Department of Labor, in a publication called *Road to High-Performance Workplaces: A Guide to Better Jobs and Better Business Results* prescribed four characteristics for which high performance workplaces should strive.[248] These characteristics were labeled "(a) skills and information; (b) participation, organization, and partnership; (c) compensation, security, and the work environment; and (d) putting it all together (5-6)." As one can easily note, the growing standard is to strive toward a high-performance workplace.[249] The development of high performance organizations is increasingly possible when all of the characteristics, constructs, and attributes expressed in this book are met.

---

[246] DeJesus, E. (2005). The human factor. *Government Computer News*, 24(19). Retrieved on April 20, 2008 from http://www.gcn.com/24_19/enterprise_software /36374-1.html?topic=enterprise_software

[247] Welbourne, T. (n.d.). High performance workplace and high performance leaders: February leadership pulse. *HR.com*. Retrieved on June, 27, 2008, from http://www.eepulse.com/ documents/pdfs/high-perf-wkplace-030804.pdf

[248] Department of Labor (DoL; 1994). *Road to high performance workplaces: A guide to better jobs and better business results*. Retrieved on January 24, 2010, from http://www.eric.ed.gov/ERICDocs/data/ericdocs2sql/ content_storage_01/0000019b/80/13/bf/4c.pdf

[249] Walsworth, S. (2005). *Globalization, high performance workplace practices and unions: Recent evidence from the Canadian workplace and employee survey*. Retrieved on June 27, 2008, from http://cerf.mcmaster.ca/ conferences/workplace05/Walsworth.pdf

This page left blank intentionally.

Success Overture

Overview

All probably should consider the association between high performance and one's bottom line as intuitive. One should obviously be able to conclude, no matter what type of entity is the focus, inefficient and ineffective processes, not delivering or achieving the desired results, or providing a terrible service, will result in a lower bottom line or financial compensation and subsequently, would not be considered as anywhere close to high performance. However, as can be observed, not every entity, be it an organization, team, individual, or leader, is high performing. So, what are some views on a value added proposition of high performance if an entity is not optimally performing?

Low or poor performance levels can cost an entity tremendously. Within an organization, if it is not continually learning and adapting to its dynamic industry because of the varying customer requirements then the customers may eventually go to another provider of services and products hoping the new company will better meet their needs. If an organization's leadership and management are so firm in their practices their employees are not being enabled to reach their full potential as well as the employees' morale and work satisfaction plummeting, the firm's retention rates could drop while employee and customer complaints increase. With the distraction of quality of leadership and management issues, the employees will only do what is asked of them and innovation will drop. This activity will then lead to quality of work issues; productions/service rates could drop while product/service quality assurance errors increase. As can been seen, the cost of low performance can have a domino effect.

So, a question one might ask is, why would all entities not strive for high performance? It is perhaps because they do not understand what it takes to be considered high performing.

Developing High Performance Organizations

Organizations consist of many different types of people, who may have different styles and who work with others they may not normally interact with on a routine basis. Organizations involve individuals, brought together, from different backgrounds and orientations. Its dynamics can prove perplexing and challenging because the members may have different values, attitudes, and expectations. Many organizations may take on their own personalities and unwritten rules frequently presenting issues for new members.

Employees and customers, all organizational stakeholders are hungry for high performance. Abraham Maslow, with his thoughts on the hierarchy of needs declared once our physical needs are met, people long for love, belonging, esteem and finally self-actualization and transcendence.[250] The psychiatrist and Holocaust survivor Viktor Frankl expounded upon this point.[251] From his experience and observations during his confinement within the concentration camps, he observed individuals believing their lives had meaning and purpose, amid the physical and emotional turmoil occurring, survived while the others perished. People and, to extrapolate, organizations want to know what they do and how they are defined actually counts and has meaning beyond the words describing the answers to these questions.

How does an organization put together a high performance team capable of meeting this challenge? As an overview, an organization should initially assess themselves. One cannot begin a journey without first knowing where one is. From the analysis of the data generated by the assessment, one should develop, author, and implement an *Organizational Effectiveness and Change Management Plan* to facilitate and guide your organization's transformation effort. The objective of *Organizational Effectiveness and Change Management* is to describe how to achieve your organization's transformation initiative to high performance. A well-coordinated and consistent change management approach is suggested to ensure your organization's personnel and stakeholders are prepared to embrace and adopt their new operating culture aligned with your organization's Strategic Plan. An *Organizational Effectiveness and Change Management Plan*, complemented by a *Strategic* and *Business Plan*, a *Strategic Communications Plan*, a *Transformation Roadmap*, and a *Performance Management Plan*, lays out a change management approach to facilitate this change and ensure the propensity for success. When developing these plans, the dimension of high performance organizations should be taken into account as well as enablers of high performance organizations while maintaining the focus on the business model of high performance organizations.

Intuitively, one can claim organizational success and organizational high performance correlates highly in a positive fashion with each other. There are some very specific characteristics of Organizational High Performance; however, the general characteristics of high performing organizations include:

- Knowing their past
- Understanding where they are

---

[250] Maslow, A. (1943). A theory of human motivation. *Psychological Review*, 50(4), 370–396. Retrieved on 25 April 2013 from http://psychclassics.yorku.ca/Maslow/motivation.htm
[251] Frankl, V. (2006). *Man's Search for Meaning. An Introduction to Logotherapy.* Boston, MA: Beacon Press.

- Focusing on a clearly defined and achievable future
- Continually learning and adapting to the environmental dynamics

In today's market, in particular for the larger industries but not necessarily limited to just them, the business environment has evolved. Gone are yesteryear business attributes of limitations and business as usual, thinking inside the box, mentality. Gone are the well-defined, hierarchical-based, structured, and traditional company, known as the Tayloristic work organization. Gone are the employees, who just do as they are told and performing routine and low-value added everyday jobs, working for a 30-year retirement pension. Here, in today's business world, there is an economy without borders, markets with worldwide labor locations, information and communications as fast as one can type because of the Internet and the Socialization Networks, and new companies led by the modern era leaders not hobbled by the past but rather being born in these modern technology-leveraging current times. Permanence and stability are not guaranteed; continual change creating flexibility and creativity is required for relevance.[252] Therefore, an organization will need to gain a competitive advantage over its competition as relevance is not a right and failure is an option.

One just needs to examine the newspapers and magazines or better yet conduct a query on their internet search engine of choice to learn there are many, once successful, organizations now failing because they did not adapt to the changing environment of their industry. One might conclude these organizations failed because they are not continuously undergoing a re-engineering or self-improvement process to lead or even just stay up with the changing times. Customers, stakeholders in general, have very little patience for an organization's substandard performance. Not an inclusive list but they want such business attributes as value for their money; low cost with high quality; and speed of delivery for as well as innovation developed variety of products, services, and expertise. Unsatisfied customers and stakeholders have very little loyalty. The bottom line is they have choices, alternatives, as to where they spend and invest their time and money. Success is not mandatory but, on the flipside of the coin, neither is mediocrity. It is up to the company's leaders, individuals, and teams to decide on their organization's fate.

It could be hypothesized no senior leadership of an organization intends to lead and manage an inferior, poor performing organization. For understanding, what would be an analogy of a poor performing organization? Imagine a boat with an incompetent coxswain who is steering the boat sometimes to the left then to the right without any apparent direction toward an objective. Additionally, in this boat,

---

[252] Duderstadt, J. (2000). *A university for the 21st century*. Ann Arbor: University of Michigan Press.

the rowers are operating at different rhythms and strengths as well as they are not rowing in the same direction. This type of organization is definitely an example of possibly the worst performing organization.

With the understanding of a poorly performing organization, what would a boat look like that is representing a high performing organization? To point out first, this type of high performing organizational boat is what all senior leaders want to develop then lead and manage. This high performing organizational boat has a competent coxswain at the rudder. This particular coxswain is steering the boat while definitively focused on the objective. The coxswain knows precisely where the boat needs to go to obtain the objective. The coxswain communicates with the rowers to ensure they understand how each needs to work in relationship with the others. The coxswain informs the rowers of the rhythm and strength with which to rower. Everyone understands their roles and responsibilities as well as what is expected of them. All of the personnel in the boat are working as a well-oiled team and will subsequently achieve the goal for which it was designed. Obviously, this analogy represents an organization performing optimally.

Age-old, sure-fire management strategies that used to work (or seemed to) now do not seem to be doing the job. Instead of improvements, many struggle to stay afloat. However, by adopting the same leadership practices used by high performance organizations, a company's performance stands a much better chance to change dramatically in a positive direction. A high performance organization is an organization achieving financial and non-financial results exceedingly better than its peer group within an industry over a set period, by focusing in a disciplined way on those matters truly important to the organization.

Knowing what a high performing organization looks like is important; however, more important is understanding why it is important. A company may not want to be high performing but success is not mandatory either. If an organization wants to optimize its profits, then it should need to be high performing as possible. A high performance organization is not created by happenstance; it is intentionally crafted through a sound methodology designed to produce an environment promoting high performance leaders, individuals, and teams.

A fundamental characteristic of high performance organizations, as mentioned earlier, is the transference from the traditional, Tayloristic work environment to regarding an organization as an innovative, holistic, and systemic entity. The organizational members, at all levels, interact and communicate with each other as they work to achieve common and accepted goals. By synergizing the Society of Human Resource Management with Gephardt and Van Buren's definition, the end state for any organization striving to become a high performance organization is:

A responsive, learning, and self-correcting organization where people, processes, and technology fully align with the organization's values, goals, and strategy as well as with its internal and external work environment and operations producing exceptional results, experiencing rapid growth, and sustaining its competitive advantage as compared to its competitors.[253] [254]

Developing High Performance Teams

The same attributes of high performance organizations form the attributes of high performance teams. High performance teams are comprised of likeminded leaders and members thinking and behaving as a collective one for the benefit of the whole. Such teams have members sharing common core goals and values aligned with the organizations strategic mission and vision. The team members and the collective team also have a clear view about their role and responsibilities toward contributing toward achieving their team's results and the organizational objectives respectively. They communicate exceptionally well within the team and to the external stakeholders and are continually learning and innovating to enable higher value-added propositions for the customers by delivering optimal products, services, and expertise. From a high-level view, to create high performance teams, leaders must transfer information, knowledge, and power to the team's membership.

A team is comprised of two or more individuals with complementary skills, interests, and beliefs brought together for coordinated activities to achieve a higher goal. They interact cooperatively and adaptively in pursuit of shared and valued objectives. Additionally, they are committed to a common purpose, work toward shared and meaningful performance goals, and take approaches for which they are mutually accountable. The team members have clearly defined and differentiated roles and responsibilities, hold task-relevant knowledge, and are interdependent.[255] [256] [257]

---

[253] Society for Human Resource Management (2007). *Business literacy glossary of terms*. Retrieved on April 3, 2012, from http://www.shrm.org

[254] Gephardt, M., & Van Buren, M. (1996). The power of high performance work systems. *Training and Development*, 50(10), 21-36.

[255] Cannon-Bowers, J., Salas, E., & Converse, S. (1993). Shared mental models in expert team decision making. In J. Castellan Jr. (Ed.), *Current issues in individual and group decision making* (pp. 221-246). Hillsdale, NJ: Erlbaum.

[256] Katzenbach, J., & Smith, D. (1993). *The wisdom of teams: Creating the high-performance organization*. Boston, MA: Harvard Business School.

[257] Morgan, B. B., Glickman, A. S., Woodward, E. A., Blaiwes, A. S., & Salas, E. (1986). *Measurement of team behaviors in a Navy environment* (Tech. Report No. NTSC TR-86-014). Orlando, FL: Naval Training Systems Center.

Teams consist of many different types of people, who may have different styles and who work with others they may not normally interact with on a routine basis. Teams may be virtual, which is often an effective way of achieving solutions but can pose challenging problems. However, because an endeavor involves individuals from different backgrounds and orientations working together to complete a common task, the team dynamics can prove perplexing and challenging. The team members may have different values, attitudes, and expectations. Many teams take on their own personalities and unwritten rules frequently present issues for new team members.

Teams comprise of organizational systems. A successful organization implies the existence of successful teams. If you accept the premise one cannot exist without the other, then the logical conclusion is organizational high performance exists because of team high performance. Similar to high performing organizations, high performance teams have both specific and general characteristics. From a high-level, the characteristics to strive for are:

- A leader
- A commitment to excellence; motivated to perform
- A clearly defined purpose
- A collaborative and transparent sense of being one instantiated via, at a minimum, effective processes and communications

The team is a function of its leader. As the leader is, so is the team. Therefore, the choice of who will be the team's leader is a critical component of the team's success. Second to deciding who the team leader is, is the leader choosing how to develop a high performance team. There are multiple paths on which to achieve team high performance. Kotter's eight-phase approach is one path that works well to develop teams with a shared vision, senior management commitment, direction, involvement, communication and processes as well as other attributes of high performance.[258] Using Lewin's methodology, which was confirmed by Moran and Brightman, to handle change management issues complements this approach.[259][260] No matter what path is chosen, the characteristics of a high performance team are:

- Situational leadership
- The team shares common goals
- Explicit and shared values supported a clear value system

---

[258] Kotter, J. (1995). Leading change: Why transformation efforts fail. *Harvard Business Review* (March-April, 1995).

[259] Lewin, K. (1947). Frontiers in group dynamics: Concept, method, and reality in social science; social equilibria, and social change. *Human Relations*, 1(1), 5-41.

[260] Moran, J., & Brightman, B. (2000). Leading organizational change. *Journal of Workplace Learning: Employee Counseling Today*, 12(2), 66-74.

- Members know their individual roles
- Pride and respect in the individual members
- Openness, trust, honesty, motivation, and enthusiasm
- Atmosphere is informal
- Everyone is included in discussions
- Conflict is not avoided but used to identify team issues
- Pride in the team and team performance
- Team information is transparent to all team members

High performance teams enable an organization to be more responsive in these modern, ever-changing, competitive environments. The members of high performance teams develop such characteristics as a shared vision, increased levels of trust and openness within the team, and continuously learn through quality leadership. Because of these and all of the other characteristics of high performance teams, results are achieved that are far greater than the sum of the individual efforts. The development of high performance teams is increasingly possible when all of the characteristics, constructs, and attributes are met.

Developing High Performance Individuals

For any endeavor successfully achieved, one must have an answer to these two simple questions. The first question defines the target to hit and the second creates the path to the target. These two questions go hand-in-hand. For example, what is the use of defining and setting a target if one never intends to take the necessary steps to hit it? Additionally, how does one set a path to a target if the target is unknown? To ensure understanding of this point, when one gets into a car to travel, the person knows two items. They know where they are and where they want to go. By knowing these two items, a leader can determine what route to take to get to where they want to go by the most effective and efficient route.

As we drill down, by turning up the magnifying intensity on the organization, we see organizations are a system of teams and high performance organizations exists because of high performance teams. Teams are organizational sub-systems comprised of individuals, the organizational human capital. To continue the argument, high performance organizations equates to high performance teams so a high performance team must have high performance individuals. The generalized definition of and thus the attributes necessary to become a high performance individual is a person who effectively applies their Knowledge, Skills, Tools, Character, and Motivation to achieve individual goals to the extent that when their efforts are combined with other individually achieved goals accomplishes Team Goals, which are necessary pieces in the process of realizing organizational goals.

Everyone has the possibility of becoming a high performance individual. Many people strive for high performance. The challenge for most people is they really do not know the answers to the two critical questions:

- What is a high performance individual?
- How do I achieve high performance?

By understanding what a high performance individual is, one can develop a roadmap to the desired target or end state. When you arrive at the target and you have become a high performance individual, one should have the mindset, behaviors, and emotions necessary to achieve your personal and professional strategic vision and goals. At the end of it all, one should have all you need to achieve success.

People, an organization's workforce, are the architectural foundation for creating a high performance organization in today's dynamic and highly competitive environment no matter the industry. How well an organization can leverage its workforce differentiates it from mediocrity to high performance.

Developing High Performance Leaders

Leaders, in general, are normally promoted based on their technical skills. At the lower supervisory levels technical skills are important; however, as a person is promoted and increases their leadership roles, their use of technical skills decreases, as they require a higher use of social skill sets.

Individuals, teams, and organizations require capable leaders, at a minimum, to guide them through the potential trials and tribulations of achieving their individual, team, or organizational strategic goals and objectives or desired end state. From a high-level overview, numerous leadership qualities need to exist for a leader, and for any other type of entity, to be considered as high performing.

A strategy toward developing high performance leaders is focused upon the end state in mind. The end state is having individuals with the attributes of high performance leaders. It is the purpose of this section to state and define those high performance leaders' attributes.

Collectively, high performance leaders are action and team oriented. There are specific activities they perform, such as:

- Providing direction, demonstrating alignment, and generating commitment as a collective leadership team
- Solving problems or making improvements efficiently and effectively through collaboration across internal or external boundaries
- Engaging employees in decision making and gaining their active support in implementing planned cross-functional actions

- Formulating joint strategies and executing them in a coordinated fashion
- Implementing successful innovation requiring cross-functional collaboration
- Adapting to change in a cohesive and coherent manner
- Working together to grow the business in new markets
- Ensuring compliance and transparency requiring a consistent set of values, beliefs and actions across the enterprise
- Being responsive to customers in ways that demand cross-unit coordination
- Developing talent on behalf of the enterprise, rather than for individual units

Some leaders may be born; however, leaders can definitely be created. All organizations deserve high performance leaders so all their employees will develop and reach the heights of their own potential. A domino effect will avail. An employee is permitted to thrive and become high performing themselves because of the existence of a high performance environment create by a high performance leader. These high performance individuals will enable the creation of high performance teams and subsequently high performance organizations.

Glossary

Action Plan: Schedule with actions, milestones, deliverables, and assigned resources to accomplish an initiative

Business Continuity Planning (BCP): This activity is the process through which organizations ensure the continuance of the mission under all conditions by establishing and exercising comprehensive continuity plans and procedures. Business Continuity Planning is critical to ensuring the organization's ability to provide timely, relevant, and valid products, services, and expertise to its stakeholders and customers.

Business Initiative Lead: The individual responsible for insuring a particular Business Initiative is achieved. Their responsibilities include, but are not limited to,

- Brief the status as well as report issues and progress of the Business Initiative to the organizational senior leaders during In-Progress Reviews (IPRs)
- Coordinate organizational representation for the Business Initiative at meetings and forums
- Coordinate with Initiative sub-leads and track their progress in accomplishing initiatives within the Business Initiative
- Approve schedules, milestones, and deliverables for initiatives are consistent with the pacing agreements

Goal: Specific, time bound statement of intended future results; how to achieve the organization's vision

Initiative: Discretionary program or project of finite duration designed to close a product, service, expertise, or performance gap

In-Progress Reviews (IPRs): An activity during which an organization's leaders are presented the status of an initiative or project

Mission: Description of the purpose of an organization; why the organization exists

Mission or Mission Area (MA): A brief statement covering, at a minimum, the purpose of the organization and its products, services, and expertise.

Objective: Specific, time bound statement of intended future results supporting a goal

PESTEL: Political, Economic, Social, Technological, Environmental, and Legal Factors

Porter's Five Forces: Power of customers, power of suppliers, threat of new entrants, threat of substitutes, and rivalry within an industry

Strategic Theme: Distinct set of related objectives, typically a vertical slice within a strategy map; often consists of a critical process for creating and delivering an organization's value

SWOT: Strengths, Weaknesses, Opportunities, and Threats

Values: Internal compass guiding an organization's and its workforce's actions; desirable thoughts, behavior, attitude, and character of the organization and its workforce

Vision: Defines the future state of the organization; where the organization is going

About the Author

Dr. Simmie A. Adams: Dr. Adams has a Bachelor of Science Degree in Psychology, a Master of Arts Degree in Counseling (Marriage and Family Therapy), and a Doctorate of Philosophy in Psychology with his area of specialization being in Industrial/Organizational Psychology. His Dissertation was on the use of Organizational Emotional Intelligence as a predictor to Organizational Performance. He is an accomplished leader with decades of experience as an Intelligence professional and Soldier.

Dr. Adams has extensive experience in both the Intelligence Community and Department of Defense (IC/DoD), ranging from direct supervisor to senior-level leadership positions. This experience has created a wealth of information to draw upon in the development, implementation, and measurement of performance oriented Business and Training Plans derived from strategic guidance. Dr. Adams' experience includes organizational development, change management, human capital management, as well as strategic plans and communications. He has strong organizational development and leadership abilities and has extensive experience in coaching, mentoring, and training personnel. Dr. Adams has strong communication skills as well as the ability to visualize issues, determine solutions, and implement decisions. He has led efforts in analyzing communications, conducting executive interviews, researching industry best practices as well as examining project issues and risks to develop performance driven strategies.

In conclusion, Dr. Adams has proven abilities in collecting and analyzing complex information to develop strategies aimed at both achieving effective transformation and desired results. His 360-degree focus on organizational issues groomed his organic knowledge base in operational and human capital environments at all levels. Dr. Adams personifies the One-Team approach in helping organizations develop strategies, which includes business and communication plans, aimed at supporting their workforces in effective transformation.

This page left blank intentionally.

This page left blank intentionally.

This page left blank intentionally.

www.ingramcontent.com/pod-product-compliance
Lightning Source LLC
Chambersburg PA
CBHW041544220426
43665CB00002B/25